Bamboo
Style

Bamboo Style

Gale Beth Goldberg

Gibbs Smith, Publisher

Salt Lake City

First Edition
06 05 04 03 02   5 4 3 2 1

Published by
Gibbs Smith, Publisher
PO Box 667
Layton, Utah 84041

Orders: (800) 748-5439
www.gibbs-smith.com

Edited by Madge Baird
Designed by Kurt Wahlner
Printed and bound in Great Britain

Library of Congress Cataloging-in-Publication Data

Goldberg, Gale Beth.

  Bamboo style / Gale Beth Goldberg ; with a foreword
by Linda Garland.— 1st ed.

    p. cm.

  ISBN 1-58685-092-X

  1. Bamboo in interior decoration. 2. Bamboo construction. 3. Bamboo. I. Title.

  NK2115.5.B36 G65 2002

  747'.9—dc21

              2001007446

Another tropical rainstorm changes from torrents to drizzle.

The heavy, dark gray clouds dissolve as an azure blue sky becomes the backdrop for the sage-green, tapering, giant grass stalks of the bamboo forest.

Heavy winds have become gentle zephyrs. Shades of jade color the bamboo culms, or stalks, and their arching branches ending in clusters of lancet-like leaves.

They speak in whispering voices: a moan, a creak, an exhalation.

A bamboo grove is a sacred place where one goes to listen, where one goes to observe the new shoots rapidly elongating as they stretch upward.

A bamboo grove is where one goes to touch the smooth, vertical fibers regularly divided and reinforced by horizontal interruptions.

Bamboo is many things to many people.

It embodies the interconnectedness of all life on this planet:

To grow and cultivate a plant that nourishes the soil, soul, and the grower.

To harvest the plant, treat it against unwanted beetles, and prepare the stock of cut culms for transport.

To distribute the readily renewable resource to the right places.

To be utilized in more than a thousand ways by skillful designers, craftspeople, manufacturers and their teams of transformers.

To be exposed to and appreciate the value of bamboo.

To have bamboo in your possession—living or crafted.

Engage actively in this inter-lifecycle and you become a part of the consciousness to sustain and preserve the earth's global resources.

Taking advantage of the versatility of bamboos in their sizes and leaf color, a low groundcover planting of Dwarf Whitestripe Bamboo *(Pleioblastus fortunei)* with white-and-green variegated leaves, creates a soft textural layer in the foreground, contrasting with a tall, dark-green-leafed Narihira Bamboo *(Semiarundinaria fastuosa)* in the background.

Dedication

To the memory of my father, Meyer Goldberg,
who, by his example, showed me the wisdom in
tzdakah (giving from the heart),
tikkun olam (repairing the world),
being an active participant in community, and teaching the next generation.

To my familial matriarch,
Ethel Shirley Rosenbluth Goldberg, and
my sibling, Dr. Lawrence H. Goldberg, who have been constant sources of
    nourishment and support.

And to the special *takenoko*—bamboo children—in my life:
    Samantha, Ryan, and Benjamin.

Contents

The taller culm with deeply carved images is a Chinese incense burner. Both endcaps have holes for the incense sticks, and the smoke wafts out through the carvings. The shorter culm is a contemporary Balinese lidded container with both surface etchings and a carved figure on the top.

At the Parq de Cafe in Montenegro, Colombia, pathways lead through several large groves of *Guadua angustifolia* bamboo.

Acknowledgments

With my spirit, I give thanks and express my gratitude. In the spirit of this bamboo book, I have merged the images of bamboo with the people who have made contributions to the creation of *Bamboo Style*.

A birth. Building a book instead of building a building.
Of love and passion, obsession and compulsion.
So many people have participated in the realization of this compilation of bamboo in so many Ways.
In gratitude, I thank

artists, artisans, architects, authors, bamboo believers, constructors, contractors, connectors, crafters, devotees, dwellers, designers, engineers, enthusiasts, experts, earthlinkage, FedExers, financial supporters (ABS, SoCal ABS, NCCABS, NEABS, EARF), furniture makers, friends, gregariousness of flowerings, growers, green doers, green gardeners, gardens, google, GS & GSP, habitués, homeowners, horticulturists, indefatigable interior designers, iron grass-vegetable steel, jewelers, knowers, lovers, landscape architects, language, manifesters, manufacturers, musicians, MACintosh experts, my magnanimous editor madge, nursery people, olam, plantations, professors, photographers, painters, pandas, the queen, rhizomatic worldwide network, sculptors, sellers, teachers all along the Way, umbrella makers, voices of bamboo speaking their bamboo truths and wisdom, writers, wonderment of bamboo, xamples, young shoots, and zealots.

Foreword by Linda Garland

Bamboo is a rising star among organic building materials. Designers who for years have been using hardwoods are becoming enchanted with the aesthetics of bamboo, a readily sustainable material for building homes, designing furniture, and crafting accessories.

Bamboo is one of nature's miracle plants. Its ratio of strength to weight is better than graphite, and it is the fastest-growing plant on earth. In the past hundred years alone, we have seen bamboo's versatility in Edison's light bulb filament, in gramophone needles, and in airplane wings.

This book is the spirit of hope and beauty, and the inspiration is bamboo.

At the turn of the twentieth century, Chippendale in England created a collection of bamboo furniture that became trendy. This gave birth to 150 bamboo-furniture factories in England. There have been other manifestations of interest in bamboo design through the years.

In 1995, a group of bamboo advocates created the backdrop for the Fourth World Bamboo Congress. Gale Goldberg and twenty others who believed in the importance of taking action worked night and day—some for years, others for months—to make the conference a reality, all of us volunteering our skills for bamboo, the timber of the future. There was a strong feeling that what we were doing was important. Some, like Gale, were inspired to take this new knowledge and create possibilities for others to learn. And so this book is born.

Many other beginnings took place at the 1995 conference in Bali. Simon Véléz, who had never left his homeland of Colombia, was invited to present his work and we were all smitten with his architectural genius. Gunter Pauli from the ZERI (Zero Emissions Research Initiative) Foundation was also in attendance, and seeds were sown for the Hannover Project, which single-hand-edly took the perception of bamboo to the level of a high-tech engineering material. German building-code officials approved the bamboo species of *Guadua* as a structural material for the ZERI Pavilion at the Hannover 2000 World's Fair. The program on the properties of bamboo in the industrial design division and furni-ture department at the Rhode Island School of Design is now in its fifth year. All of these foundations have added to the understanding of the appropriate use of the material.

My fascination with bamboo started as a child in Ireland, where the Gulf Stream allowed us to have tropical gardens. Later, in the early 1970s in Bali, where I had made my home, I grabbed onto the outrigger of a fisherman's boat as I surfaced from a dive. To my surprise, the outrigger turned out to be a species of giant timber bamboo. I convinced the fisherman to take me to the forest where the boatmen harvested their bamboo poles. I will never for-get the first time I saw those giants—nearly ten inches in diameter and a hundred feet tall—overlapping in Gothic arches almost like a jungle cathedral. And so my bamboo journey started.

The first step was a furniture collection that I created and used in many projects over the years. You may have seen the furni-ture in the *Architectural Digest* issues on Richard Branson's island, Necker; David Bowie's house on Mustique; and Ian Fleming's house in Jamaica, which is now owned by Chris Blackwell. My bamboo pieces can be found in castles in Scotland, palaces in India, and beach houses in Fiji. Across the globe, the beauty of these giants continues to captivate.

And so we continue. I love what Gale is adding to this tapes-try that has for thousands of years continued to be contemporary. It is my hope that, after being inspired by her bamboo journey, you, too, will join the ever-growing family of believers.

Linda Garland is the founder of the Environmental Bamboo Foundation, Bali, Indonesia, and the "Queen of Bamboo."

Introduction

The human form and spirit would have much to emulate in the power of bamboo: standing upright, yet strong and supple; being flexible yet resilient in light of nature's forces; being grounded with an extensive rootedness to the earth yet light and airy in response to the slightest breeze.

The Asian cultures admire, respect, and honor the beauty of bamboo—a super-fast-growing and self-renewing plant. With a few simple tools, this amazing grass, so rich in its diversity, is easily shaped into more than a thousand uses, some of which are detailed below:

- Bamboo scaffolding is split and fastened to building façades by lashing lengths together to secure the necessary support to build the building higher. Hong Kong high-rises are wrapped with a bamboo framework that eases the steel building's construction and exterior maintenance. These structures are breathtaking when viewed through an intricate web—a basket of bamboo.

- Bamboo creates music. In a range of forms, bamboo becomes musical instruments, from the slit drum and marimba played by the Bamboo Orchestra of Japan to the pan flutes and the thin sliver that is shaped into a vibrating reed for melodious notes of many wind instruments—a saxophone, clarinet, and oboe; a Balinese *tingklik* (a bamboo xylophone) is played in the gamelan percussion orchestra. A Japanese *shakuhachi* is a type of flute made from the bamboo rhizome, the underground stem. An Australian Aboriginal didgeridoo is a long and large hollowed bamboo horn. A rain stick is a percussion instrument—a seed-filled hollow tube of bamboo—originally made and used in Chile and Africa.

- Before paper was made and used, the Chinese wrote books on bamboo strips an inch or two wide that were joined together with fine silk threads. Now, bamboo pulp is formed into textured paper.

- A slender bamboo stalk becomes a writing implement for bamboo poetry or an ink brush for Japanese *sumi-e* (bamboo paintings).

- Tender spring bamboo shoots add a flavorful crunch and crispy texture to a Chinese banquet. Bamboo beer is a refreshing fermented drink.

- A Chinese herbal remedy used for kidney distress is formulated from a combination of the underground stem of the black bamboo (*Phyllostachys nigra*) and other plant ingredients.

- The "tabasheer" of some tropical bamboos—a white, crystalline silica substance secreted on the inside surface of the stalk between the nodes, or divisions—has been used to treat bronchial ailments and has a reputation of being an aphrodisiac.*

*Marden, Luis, "Bamboo, the Giant Grass," *National Geographic*, October 1980, p. 515.

Historical Uses

More than a thousand years ago, the Japanese assimilated elements of Chinese culture into their own. While the Chinese use bamboo in engineered structures, the Japanese favor the beauty of bamboo in ornamentation and decoration, as well as for use in ritual ceremonies.

Tortoiseshell bamboo (*Phyllostachys pubescens* var. *heterocycla*), with its nodes climbing alternately up the culm (stalk) at nearly forty-five-degree angles, is treasured for its unusual character and is formed into flower vases, plant pots, and lamp bases.

In the Japanese home, woven bamboo creates patterned ceilings, forms moldings and trims, and is often positioned as a single column located in an auspicious corner. Chairs, benches, and tables are consciously designed with a "bamboo aesthetic"—simple, clean lines, Zen-like and sparse, sensitive to the natural bent of bamboo. A fine, skillfully shaped bamboo whisk whips the froth in the traditional Japanese tea ceremony.

Outside the home, bamboo fences delineate and decorate. Sometimes they provide privacy; at other times, the open weave of tied culms becomes an artistic vertical divide separating garden paths and plantings.

The Asians are not alone in demonstrating the multiple uses of bamboo. In another part of the bamboo world—Colombia, South America—giant bamboo timbers bolted together in triangulated architectural trusses are so strong that they can freely span more than eighteen feet (six meters) while supporting a heavy roof of cement, steel mesh, and clay tile. Thinner bamboos can be a woven basket inside a greenhouse or attached between ceiling rafters, forming a herringbone pattern.

In Ecuador, architects and builders are designing innovative and affordable housing constructed of bamboo. Full bamboo culms are flattened and their nodes (horizontal joints) scraped clean. Panels of these crushed bamboo culms span between wooden supports, forming the building's exterior skin. In another creative solution, a pool pavilion's hyperbolic roof is shaped with sturdy bamboo poles.**

At Catholic University in Brazil, the health-care industry is benefiting from creative designs of lightweight and strong bamboo walkers for both children and seniors.***

Where and How Bamboo Grows

Bamboo grows prolifically between the Tropics of Cancer and Capricorn. Some tropical culms are as thick as a plantation worker's thigh. From deep within the bamboo forest, tapering stalks arch toward each other, creating a shade canopy of delicate leaves and branches. Here, only small patches of filtered sunlight reach the ground where the spring shoots grow.

**Darrel DeBoer presentation, American Bamboo Society Conference, Portland, Oregon, September 2001.
***Ibid.

The physiology of this remarkable plant is complex. Technically, it is a grass. Depending on growing conditions, some species stay low to the ground, reaching only six to twelve inches high. Other giant grasses tower above at heights of more than a hundred feet. Some plants are pencil-thin; others have diameters of nearly a foot. Some are hollow between the nodes; others are solid. Some gracefully grow tall and straight; others are irregularly shaped with crooks and bends and alternating humps, much like the protective shells turtles carry with them.

Unlike woody trees that grow bigger around each year, a bamboo shoot emerges from the ground with its thickness fixed. The culm spends a single season of growing time—about six weeks—elongating like a telescope (wider at the base and midsection, tapering at the top) to its full height and development.

The dominant colors of these extended bamboo poles are shades of green. Certain species have surfaces that are yellow, purple, brown, or black. Other culms stand out in appearance with their blotchy spots, striped stalks, or variegated leaves.

The colorful immature culm is protected with a heavy, leafy covering called a sheath, which contains growth hormones used by the maturing plant. At maturity, the sheath drops off and becomes nutritious mulch. After the bamboo stalk has finished its vertical growth extension, branches and leaves form at the nodes. Bamboo is strengthened by these horizontal joints (nodes), which are spaced at regular intervals six to eighteen inches apart.

While trees contain cellulose fibers that are made only of lignin, bamboos contain cellulose fibers with lignin and silica—the same hard, glassy substance found in sand, and a big factor in bamboo's high density, strength, and hardness. Bamboo fibers are nearly ten times as long as those found in trees.*

During bamboo's growth activity aboveground, the rhizomes, or underground stems, are also busy. The gnarly, dense network with smaller intertwining roots spreads to create a strong foundation in a growing zone found about two to three feet below the soil's surface.

The underground structure of the rhizomes determines whether bamboo is grouped into the category of "clumper" or "runner." *Clumpers* sprout a new shoot from a tightly spaced rhizome and root system. *Runners* send out extensive lengths of rhizomes that can pierce the ground surface many yards away from their origin.

Dedicated researchers have identified more than a thousand species grouped in over a hundred genera. They rely on the flowering of the bamboo to name the species. The infrequent flowering of bamboos, however, makes the process of identification difficult. Some bamboos bloom once every thirty years, while others can take a century to produce flowers and seeds. Surprisingly, bamboos of the same species can bloom simultaneously around the globe—gregarious flowering—and then die. Some bamboos flower often and do not die. These unusual life-cycle patterns of growth add complexity to the study of bamboos.

*Walter Liese, *Bamboos—Biology, silvics, properties, utilization*, p. 73.

Bamboo's Journey

Many Southeast Asian cultures revere and respect bamboo, honoring the material in spirit through traditional ceremonies. The Japanese, Chinese, Balinese, Indian, Filipino, Thai, and Vietnamese peoples weave wondrous stories in music and poetry about bamboo's nature and aesthetics. Bamboo is also significant in the lives of these people, who have not only recognized its uses but also appreciated and depended upon its economic value for generations.

For more than a century, the sojourn of bamboo from the Asian Pacific countries east to the shores of the United States has brought furniture, furnishings, decorative objects, and fine art. Other useful objects include kitchenware, baskets, trays, wind chimes, umbrellas, flutes, and fans. Fences and gazebos, sheds and shelters, sacred and ceremonial spaces are among the bamboo structures that have been adapted to Western living.

Travelers from the West observe and appreciate how bamboo is transformed into beautiful shapes and forms. Artisans learn traditional and modern techniques used by the masters in Eastern cultures to make useful bamboo objects.

Increasingly large quantities of finished bamboo products that are packed in containers and shipped across the ocean continue to have a positive economic impact on the Pacific Rim countries. Today the contents of the containers include manufactured flooring, ply-bamboo, paneling, fencing, woven matting, window coverings, furniture, and accessories. Western designers are creating artistic environments that contribute to a fashionable "bamboo style" in contemporary settings.

Knowing Bamboo

Increased environmental awareness is a major factor in bamboo's growing popularity. Designers, builders, and clients are paying attention to how we can protect the integrity of our world. The "green" building movement promotes *sustainability*, where resources are used in a holistic and responsible way that considers the future as well as the present, and where lessons learned from the past are practiced today.

Bamboo regenerates quickly, replacing nearly a third of its biomass (living matter per unit volume of habitat) annually. In a three- to five-year time frame, bamboo fibers mature and culms can be harvested. Compare the growth pace of bamboo with a soft- or hardwood forest, which takes about fifty to sixty years to reach maturity. Harvested and treated bamboo can be put into use in one-tenth the time it takes for a tree to be felled and milled. This hardy, fast-growing, strong, flexible, and beautiful grass has great potential to supplement the use of timber in our buildings and furnishings. Presently, rigorous scientific testing of bamboo's structural properties and the development of internationally recognized building codes are encouraging safe and creative building with bamboo in the Americas, Europe, and Asia.

About the Author

Bamboo is an extension of the people in the Asian cultures. This natural symbiosis on so many levels has been a grassroots influence on Americans and bamboo. The beauty of bamboo and the beauty of people growing and working with bamboo are what got me started.

The Japanese practice of cutting a child's umbilical cord with a bamboo knife, a practice reserved for nobility, is said to bless the child with a life of happiness. While my cord wasn't cut that way, I feel that bamboo has brought significant happiness to my life and has greatly influenced my path.

I had practiced as an architect on both the east and west coasts for almost fifteen years before I met bamboo and began to develop a relationship with it. This attraction took me to parts of the world I had never been: Bali, Costa Rica, and Colombia.

In 1995, at the Fourth World Congress on Bamboo and Bamboo Festival in Bali, I first saw architect Simón Vélez's photographs of his fantastic and fascinating bamboo constructions hanging in the great space of Linda Garland's bamboo estate and presented in slides at the conference. Linda asked me to take charge of all the documentation at the Bamboo Festival—photography, audio- and videotapings. Assisted by more than twenty volunteers, I gathered prints, slides and recordings that provided a record of the extraordinary event. I returned home to southern California wanting to learn more about bamboo. In 1998, I received support from the Chicago-based Graham Foundation for Advanced Studies in the Fine Arts, and traveled to Bogotá, Colombia, to study bamboo building with Vélez and his artisan- and builder-colleague Marcelo Villegas. I wrote a story about bamboo architecture in Colombia, which included more than a hundred photographs, and self-published the report. Since then, I've been studying this amazing plant from the inside out. During 2000, I began to share this information at bamboo events and workshops, and on the World Wide Web. Each day, I continue to learn more and more about bamboo and its possibilities—through Internet discussion groups, books, articles, and conversations with bamboo experts. I have participated in bamboo building workshops; attended regional, national, and international bamboo conferences; given presentations about Simón Vélez and his bamboo architecture; specified bamboo flooring in several architectural projects; and consulted with clients about growing bamboo, drawing on my undergraduate background in landscape architecture.

I am eager to share what I know, to educate and teach people about bamboo, from the folks next door to those in positions of influence. I have visions and ambitions for the broadened use of bamboo in a civilized world that is looking for sustainability and viability. There is potential to establish bamboo plantations at wastewater treatment sites, which would create a symbiosis of great advantage. The homeless and less privileged could be trained to work with bamboo—planting, growing, harvesting, seasoning, and treating the canes. They could develop skills to build with bamboo and then be sheltered by their own creations.

I want to give everyone the opportunity to become familiar with bamboo as a living plant and as a material that can be used for so many things. I am an enthusiast for bamboo, its role on the planet, its possibilities, its challenges, and its rewards. With the dedication of others, I share their bamboo designs for living—from a carved bamboo writing pen to a restaurant where bamboo planks cover the floor, walls, and ceiling.

I hope that your own bamboo journey will take you to many places. I encourage you to bring bamboo into your life, and to take this book along as a guide and reference for that adventure.

About This Book

Bamboo's growing popularity in today's marketplace is exciting and offers enormous possibilities for people around the world who design and build with bamboo. While this book provides a basic introduction to the extensive and deeply rooted role that bamboo plays for more than half of the globe's population, and outlines traditional and historical uses of bamboo in Asian cultures and other Pacific Rim populations, its main thrust is on bamboo in contemporary environments, both indoors and outdoors. It features products manufactured with bamboo, including flooring, furniture, and accessories. The exceptional work of several bamboo artisans is highlighted. Two chapters outline how to grow and harvest bamboo (it can be grown almost anywhere in the world) and how to craft useful and decorative items from it. All of these examples are meant to inspire you to create your own unique place where bamboo becomes integral with your lifestyle choices.

This book could be considered an initial foundation for the bamboo novice, as well as an idea book for the home designer. But there is so much more to learn about bamboo than I can begin to explain here. A considerable number of books, articles, and conference proceedings are referenced throughout the text. A plentiful bibliography and ample resources direct you to places where you can enrich your understanding.

Choose bamboo and you will be forever changed.

Why Choose Bamboo?

One of the main questions presented in the Environmental Bamboo Foundation's literature is "Why bamboo?" along with some answers: bamboo is versatile and has a short growth cycle, it is a high-yield, renewable resource for agroforestry products. A few more answers follow.

More Than a Thousand

There are almost as many reasons to choose bamboo as there are numbers of species, uses, and ways to put this magical material together. Westerners who are most familiar with bamboo use in tropical areas might be surprised to know that between one-third and one-half of the world's population integrates bamboo into their basic lifestyles. In cultures where bamboo groves serve the population as indigenous timber, local growers, harvesters, artisans, and builders have contributed enormously to the socioeconomic development of their regions.

Four-to-six-inch-diameter timber bamboos make up this triangulated roof truss. Smaller, one-to-two-inch-diameter bamboos create a linear-patterned infill between the upper rafter chords. A bamboo cathedral ceiling and structure is strong and sturdy. It carries the weight of the heavy clay tile of the roof and the lightweight steel-strength bamboo framework.

The form and materials used to make one of three bamboo tepees built at the Bamboo Festival in Bali could be easily adapted in a bamboo backyard just about anywhere. A woven thatch is wrapped around the tepee framework. The dirt floor is made warmer and softer underfoot with a bas-ket-weave-pattern bamboo rug.

A few of the more than one thousand items currently made from bamboo include arbors and arrows, baskets and bicycles, candlesticks and cradles, domes and dowels, eggcups, fans and flutes, gates and gutters, hats and headrests, incense, jewelry, kites, ladders and ladles, masts and mobiles, nails and needles, organs, paper and pipes, quivers, rakes and reeds, surfboards and stools, tepees and torches, umbrellas, valances and vaults, walkers, wheelchairs, waterwheels and windmills, xylophones, yurts, zephyrs and zithers.

More Than a Million

People's lives in China, Japan, India, Indonesia, Philippines, Thailand and Vietnam are intrinsically woven with bamboo. The Chinese respect and honor bamboo as a friend to humankind. To compromise, to yield, to continue ahead despite obstacles is the Japanese bamboo way.

To the Pacific Rim cultures, the nature of bamboo represents strength, flexibility, and longevity. Symbolically, bamboo represents dependability and endurance.

It is supple, elastic, and tenacious.

Bamboo is a survivor: it bends but does not break.

Some of the world's largest populations live where bamboo is abundant, and they harvest the plant for use in buildings, furniture, crafts, decorative arts, musical instruments, and kitchen utensils. These Far Eastern cultures have grown, harvested, and put this giant grass to use in thousands of ways for thousands of years.

A sampling of antique woven Japanese bamboo baskets available at Maienza Wilson design gallery.

Their traditions include using bamboo to build houses for their families, shelters for their animals, and fences for their backyards. They make simple, elegant, and practical furniture: chairs, sofas, chaise longues, benches, tables, hutches, cabinets and such.

In comparison to bamboo, brick and concrete and steel are recognized as long-lasting building materials. Multistory structures built from steel, concrete and brick can endure for several centuries. These materials are also much heavier and more expensive to manufacture and transport. Bamboo's local availability and its light weight—due to being mostly hollow along its length—make it a very cost-effective building material.

Viewing the bamboo grove beyond, one sees in the foreground an image of a handsome harvested bamboo trellis edging a pathway next to a low, mounding variety of living bamboo. All these bamboo variations are more than enough encouragement for one to travel to the French home of a bamboo nursery—La Bambouseraie in Prafrance.

Because bamboo is relatively easy to cultivate, quick to grow and mature, and fairly easy to harvest, cure, and season for the marketplace, it is becoming more and more visible in the building industry. An international group of designers admire and promote bamboo as a renewable building resource—an alternative to old-growth northern, southern, and rain-forest hardwoods. One example is internationally acclaimed Colombian bamboo architect Simón Vélez, who designs earthquake-safe housing as well as large ranches, estates, family compounds, resorts, and public pavilions.

Bamboo Socioeconomics

The resurgence of interest in bamboo—a bamboo renaissance—stems partly from our increased environmental and ecological awareness. We recognize the limited resources of our planet and are looking towards materials that can be replenished and also make socioeconomic sense.

A bamboo corral holds livestock within bounds, and a bamboo roof structure supports the heavy clay tiles with triangulated trusses.

The indigenous peoples in less-developed nations located in the tropical zone have truly been lucky that bamboo is abundant. The same bamboo that is used to protect people from harsh climatic conditions is also used to provide shelter for livestock. The rural dwellers create a range of shelters, often rudimentary, single-story bungalows whose main bamboo columns are dug straight into the ground.

Bamboo structures built this way have a limited life span of about five years. But they can be easily rebuilt with new growth that's been harvested, cured, and treated and is ready for use in about the same amount of time.

A collection of bamboo products available in the marketplace is found at the eclectic shop Scavenge: bamboo umbrellas, woven bamboo hats, rain sticks, tiki torches, and candles made from full culms.

The marketing of bamboo products has benefited both those who make the goods and those who buy them. With the advent of the Internet and the resulting active worldwide marketplace, available bamboo products range from antique and contemporary Oriental arts and crafts, to bamboo-composite building materials and bamboo paper goods.

When the wealthy want bamboo as much as, or even more than, a third of the world's population has wanted bamboo for many generations—both for socioeconomic growth and for survival—then the consciousness levels and awareness of the versatile virtues of bamboo will increase, as will its presence.*

*Professor Walter Liese of Hamburg University, Germany, "Opportunities and Constraints for Processing and Utilization of Bamboo and Rattan in North-East India," paper delivered for the International Fund for Agricultural Development, February 22–23, 2001, Rome, Italy.

Bamboo is currently being elevated to a substantial stature in architecture and high-end furniture and furnishings. Antique bamboo pieces that create a Zen feeling in an environment are highly valued in the U.S., as seen in a rug-merchant's window, a design gallery, a minimalist meditation space, or an upscale house remodel.

Through the window of the Maienza Wilson design gallery, one's eye can focus on several bamboo designs: the table base by Budji with an inverted woven tray top, a woven basket, vertical timber bamboo poles that separate the window display space from the rest of the gallery, and small-diameter bent-bamboo horizontal poles that support the hanging tapestry.

Building Anew with Bamboo

Structural bamboo roof rafters and framed walls are combined with native woods—coconut palms in Bali and mangrove, arboloco, and macana in Colombia, to name a few—to create housing and other structures in several tropical countries.

The National Housing Project in Costa Rica (mid-1990s–2000) was an example of the efficient use of bamboo in construction. They established an active plantation where bamboo was cultivated, cut, cured and seasoned. When it was ready, they used the bamboo to build low-cost residences. Under dedicated leadership and the vision of two Costa Rican architects, Cecilia Chavez and Jorge Gutierrez, and with

This consciously holistic custom Hawaiian bamboo house built by Bamboo Technologies sits on a raised platform wrapped with a skirt of bamboo. The porch promenade has several sections of bamboo railing made of vertical and horizontal pieces. With a sensitive and careful eye, the designers integrated the interesting shape of the rhizome ends of the harvested bamboo stalks into the detail of the column brackets.

Included with Bamboo Technologies' prefabricated houses are wall panels with exterior bamboo siding and interior woven bamboo finish, roof panels overlaid with three-quarter-inch bamboo plywood, and a queen-size bamboo bed. Available options include bamboo flooring, bamboo kitchen counters and cabinets, a bamboo bathroom vanity, and bamboo light fixtures, switches, and receptacle covers. Even custom-woven textures and patterns for the wall and roof panels can be specified.

the help of designers and constructors, they were approaching the goal of building nearly a thousand houses per year.

In other parts of the world, building with bamboo is part of the culture.

- A teahouse constructed mostly of bamboo is a sacred space in China.
- A bungalow in Hawaii may be crafted from bamboo.
- The walls of an art studio in northern California are built with straw bales and the roof is built with bamboo trusses.

The bamboo wall panels, the eaves frieze, and the walkway railing are designed in simple, rhythmic and repetitious patterns that add to the peaceful sacredness of this teahouse in China.

New outdoor constructions of bamboo—trellises, pergolas, garden shade structures—provide protection from the elements.

For a long time, bamboo has been associated with tropical settings and South Seas clichés like tiki huts. While a certain bamboo style still evokes this laid-back, relaxed vacation mode replete with a bamboo umbrella garnish in the Mai Tai, there are talented and skillful designers and craftspeople who are creating pieces from laminated bamboo that's been bent and shaped. Definitely modern, these chairs and tables fit comfortably into contemporary settings.

From a beachside public vista in southern California, one catches a glimpse of a bamboo garden gazebo, a shady shelter for visiting or lunching. Multiple living bamboos create a backdrop that towers at least twenty feet in the air.

A variety of furniture and furnishing styles make up the global bamboo marketplace. Today, traditional designs and modern interpretations by furniture makers can be found in high-end design showrooms and local swap meets. These range from large-scale timber bamboos crafted into living room sofas, lounge chairs and low tables, to four-poster beds flanked by night tables with lamps whose bases and shades are made of bamboo. Woven and plaited bamboos are made into wall paneling, room dividers, window shades, and floor mats. Bamboo tableware, serving spoons, bowls, and trays adorn living room, altar, buffet, and dining room tables, as well as bookcases and armoires.

We are surrounded by bamboo integrated into interesting designs. Artistic expressions of bamboo in pen-and-ink or watercolors often have an inherent spiritual quality. Woven baskets, carved tea whisks, vases, ladles, fans, trivets, and toys are a sampling of functional and sculptural bamboo crafts.

Made completely of laminated, bent, and shaped bamboo, this sleek side chair and table are designs by architect Michael McDonough. The curvaceous interlocking and slotted table base panels demonstrate designing with bamboo in a sophisticated style. The circular tabletop is also laminated bamboo with a full bull-nosed rounded shape that softens the edge.

Talented craftsman Jo Scheer designed and built this sweet bamboo porch swing where one can take in the lush surroundings and wind down the day with a cool tropical drink. The porch railing is a lovely designed and executed interweaving of split bamboo strips.

Small, medium, and tall dresser/ storage units are framed in wood with split bamboo insets on the tops, sides, and drawer fronts. Available at Pier 1 Imports.

A few simple bamboo touches add to this place setting: bamboo-handled flatware, a bamboo place mat, and a turned-bamboo vase. Available at William Laman.

Thời Trang
112 CẦU GIẤY

A shopkeeper's bamboo rack stylishly displays hats for women and men.

Remodeling, Too, with Bamboo

Contemporary interior living spaces that are reconstructed using manufactured bamboo products invite inquiries. Designers and homeowners alike, taking notice of bamboo's beauty and sensing a different quality to the material, want to know: What type of wood is that? Is it a "green" product? Where can I get it? Is it affordable?

Similar to manufactured wood products, some bamboo products use the entire culm and branches. Bamboo chips, strips, and sawdust glued under pressure make particleboard, flake board, and oriented strand board (BOSB).

DENSITY	RELATIVE STABILITY	DURABILITY
Bamboo's hardness factor (measured in pounds per square inch) is similar to maple and oak.	Bamboo is twice as stable as red oak.	Bamboo's durability depends on proper maintenance, similar to any hardwood floor. To keep bamboo flooring looking good and lasting long, clean and refinish periodically.
Plyboo® 1130-1400 PSI Red Oak 1290 PSI Teak 1000 PSI	Plyboo® .00175 Red Oak .00369 Teak .00186	

Other manufactured items, like bamboo plywood and flooring, are formed from bamboo strips. They are cut and planed from whole timber-sized culms, which are then laminated together. Ply-bamboo sheet goods come in familiar building dimensions, typically measuring two feet by six feet. Composites made from layers of bamboo laminates are fabricated into finished floors, cabinetry, and stylish furniture.

Bamboo flooring is rapidly becoming recognized as a healthy, renewable, "green," and attractive alternative to hardwood flooring. Bamboo compares favorably to hardwoods in cost, density, and durability.

Striking in its uniformity and modern application, Plyboo is fashioned into cabinet displays and wall-covering backdrops for the artistic expressions at Micaela's gallery in San Francisco.

An attractive interior décor combines bamboo elements from floor to ceiling: a horizontally laminated and prefinished bamboo plank floor, a baseboard made of bamboo, a woven bamboo screen, or a framed fabric screen with an artist's bamboo brush strokes depicting a bamboo grove. A natural bamboo vase here, a grouping of amber bamboo candles there, a celadon ceramic pot housing a beautiful living bamboo specimen. We enjoy the privacy a bamboo window shade gives and we admire a bamboo curtain rod supporting a natural fabric drapery. We look up at the ceiling and discover small bamboo pieces fitted snugly between bamboo roof rafters.

An effective bamboo ambiance can be a collection of many things bamboo—in the architectural structure, interior finishes, furniture, furnishings, decorative objects, and accessories.

A simple and straightforward lantern is crafted from split bamboo strips, woven together with even thinner and more flexible bamboo splits secured to a black metal rod framework. The bamboo vision is enhanced with the potted bamboo plants that sit on the deck outside the window.

The colored waxes were poured into a mold made of bamboo culms and formed into fabulous tapers. These candles take on the variety of shapes found in living bamboo: evenly spaced nodes about six inches apart, regularly spaced shorter interruptions about three-to-four inches apart, and swollen nodes in a golden-colored waxed version.

33

Aesthetics of Bamboo

Ideas of bamboo design and construction weave together the material's physical strength and its aesthetic qualities. Bamboo is a remarkable construction material. It's sturdy and flexible. Its mass-to-weight ratio is high, meaning that there's a lot of substance and little weight. This is a highly desirable quality in a building material, making the "work" of a structural component very efficient.

Bamboo is Strong.

- It has greater strength than steel in tension.

- It is stronger than concrete in compression.

Split bamboo is the outermost wrapping around this built-up construction of a tall, vertical rhizome culm and two short bamboo supports that cradle culms running horizontally. The closely spaced nodes at the lower section of the rhizome culm are penetrated by two horizontal reinforcing culms. The whole combination exudes strength.

Located south of Bogotá, Colombia, Simón Vélez designed this marketplace using multi-stalked, triangulated *Guadua* bamboo roof trusses. The roof cantilever extends the length of "three Simon's" (nearly twenty feet). Over Simon's shoulder, the dense grove of *Guadua* has a feathery canopy of lush green leaves.

Bamboo is Flexible.

A Japanese sleeve fence (*sodi-gaki*) takes its top chord curved shape from many thin, plaited split strips made from a giant timber bamboo and recombined.

- Its vertical columnar fibers move in gentle breezes or strong winds—bending with the circumstances. It shoulders the weight of winter snows. When warm weather thaws the snow, the bamboo springs back.

- It can be bent, woven, curved, shaped, molded, or laminated. When it is transformed from a whole or split culm, it becomes the art, the object of the art, and the tool of the art.

- It flexes physically whether it's a whole-culm roof rafter or a split-culm deck railing.

Bamboo splits are fastened together to create a woven tree house railing designed and built by Jo Scheer. Three suspended sculptures demonstrate the flexible interweavings of bamboo: a ball of bamboo that mostly isn't there, a potted plant hanger secured at the ends and splayed in the middle, and a pair of interlocking triangles.

Bamboo is Beautiful.

- It is a simple, elegant, and smooth cylinder between the nodes.

- When growing, its colors range in many shades of green, blue, and yellow. It is interesting in appearance with variegated stripes—green on a yellow background and yellow on green.

- After it has been cut, its natural cured colors range in shades of khaki. Treat it with heat torching, torching and staining, or cooking-drying-dyeing and the range of colors is a full rainbow spectrum.

- It comes in different shapes and sizes. It can be a ground cover, low hedge, or a tall and dense living fence. Its stalks can be straight or zigzag or tortoiseshell-shaped. Many large-diameter whole culms joined together can support a building's roof or make a canopy bed. Many small-diameter culms bundled together can form a table leg or a porch column.

- It is a giant grass that can be joined together in triangular configurations, such as in a roof truss, a bridge, or a sculpture.

Split bamboo is artistically woven into an elegantly shaped traditional Japanese bamboo basket. Available at Mingei gallery.

Some *Phyllostachys aureosulcata* culms grow in a crooked, zigzag form that adds visual interest.

A kitchen bar countertop designed by "green" contractor Joe Campanelli for his construction office is a weaving of laminated bamboo flooring—vertical and horizontal, honey and amber colored—inlaid with Chinese coins.

This gorgeous clump of yellow bamboo (*Schizostachyum brachycladum*) located on Linda Garland's property is artistically set apart as a focal point in the otherwise lush tropical landscape. The stalks grow out of a mound of black, washed river stones that form an attractive and contrasting composition.

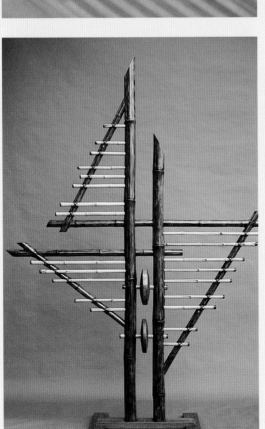

Calvin Hashimoto named his sculpture *Abacus*, derivative of the carved coconut "counters" suspended in the middle of the bamboo sculpture. The small horizontal bamboos imply the graduated denominations in an abstract sense. "The composition embodies the mystery of mathematics, which starts as a science but in its furthest extension opens the door to the spiritual," explains Hashimoto.

Bamboo is
Renewable.

- It is attractive to builders, designers, and crafters because it's a renewable plant that, after harvest, can be treated non-toxically against insects.

- It grows in groves with a substantial foundation consisting of a network of underground rhizome stems and roots that regenerate themselves.

Mature *Guadua* grove at
Parq de Cafe in
Montenegro, Colombia.

Bamboo is Sustainable.

- It is a plant that sustains itself on its own; yet it benefits from routine cutting. Sustainability can be thought of as a way of being holistically responsible at the local, grassroots level—with a global effect.

- It is an ancient plant. Like corn to the Aztecs and rice to the Asians, bamboo has been a staple in many cultures of the world. Friendly to the environment, bamboo's own compost fertilizes the next generation—the leaves and branches decompose, nourishing the soil below.

- Because bamboo renews rapidly, it can help protect and preserve the environment for current and future generations. Ideally, the speed of a material's regeneration matches the need for its utilization.

- As the rate of bamboo processing increases, it is important that producers be conscious of the increasing demand. Just as important, the high quality of bamboo in the marketplace must be consistent.

- How our actions and choices affect both our local communities and those beyond our boundaries must be considered. A balance must be maintained that does not exploit one over the other. How bamboo grows and sustains itself represents an inter-life cycle of regenerative ecology. Respect of traditional time-tested methods that work together with innovative new technologies can help achieve solid solutions for today and for tomorrow.*

*From the Introduction to *The Parade of Green Buildings*, a pamphlet published by The Sustainability Project and the Santa Barbara Contractors Association for their event in October 2000, p. 5.

Bamboo is Workable.

- Builders use bamboo for structures—dwellings, sheds, bridges, and fences.

- Structures designed using cut bamboo culms as vertical supports can bounce and dance, easily responding to the seismic movement of the earth. Consequently, bamboo is often the choice for building in earthquake-prone zones around the world. Bamboo domes and geodesic structures can provide temporary, post-disaster shelters. A kit of parts—cut bamboo, bolts and fasteners, tools, and a material to cover the framework—can be air-dropped and assembled quickly and easily.

- Craftspeople and designers create with whole and split culms. Skilled artists build furniture—tables, chairs, lounges, and beds. A few examples of bamboo furnishings are light fixtures, window shades, wall panels, and floor mats.

Above: A bamboo hassock is woven from different sizes of split bamboos, creating light and dark patterns.
Left: Full *Guadua* culms are used for the walking surface and handrails in the design of this footbridge at the Parq de Cafe in Colombia.
Facing: Wardrobe doors designed by Beverly Messenger are made with a bamboo ladder-grid tied with black-dyed hemp and combined with reed matting. The woven seat and back of a timber-bamboo chair from Bali has both wrapped and fitted joints. A Buddha, crafted bamboo objects, a Balinese umbrella, and a bamboo-motif fabric on the wall define her altar niche.

Bamboo is Durable.

- To increase the longevity of bamboo as a material for all its many and varied uses, culms are best cut six weeks prior to use while they are still pliable and easily worked.

- Cut bamboo, if left untreated and unprotected, will deteriorate quickly—in two to three years. However, if one takes precautions, the material can be serviceable for ten, twenty, or even fifty to a hundred years. The Chinese temples, Japanese homes, and ceremonial teahouses last a long time because the highly regarded cut culms receive a good *hat*, a good *jacket*, and a good pair of *boots*.

- A good *hat* acts like an umbrella. Some examples of a good hat: the buildings on Linda Garland's Panchoran property in Bali have generous roof eaves and gabled ends overhanging the main bamboo structure, effectively shedding the often-torrential rains; and Simón Vélez and Marcelo Villegas's roof "sombreros" prevent the intense rays of the sun from directly penetrating the buildings, keeping them comfortably cool with only nature's air conditioning.

A rural residence in Colombia designed and built by artisan Marcelo Villegas has a splayed bamboo roof rafter and triangulated-truss support system. It is protected by the red-clay-tile roofing on top of several inches of a concrete-impregnated expanded metal mesh roof diaphragm. The broad roof overhang—a wide-brimmed *hat*—not only keeps the bamboo below dry, but direct sun penetration is also prevented.

- A good *jacket* acts like a slicker—repelling the rain. Bamboo culms have their own protective resins that come to the surface when heated, which then can be rubbed to a lovely sheen. This natural protective shield can break down over time if exposed to too much direct sunlight. Several coatings of a protective liquid sealer, reapplied periodically, can help buffer the sun's effects on the bamboo's exposed outermost layer. Depending on specific microclimate conditions, reapplication of the protection may be needed more or less frequently. Applying a thick, rich coating of lacquer, varnish, resin, or polyurethane will reduce the deleterious bleaching and cracking effects of the sun for fences, outdoor furniture, and structures.

- A good pair of *boots* will prevent the wicking up of water. In construction use, the cut ends of bamboo are vulnerable if in direct contact with water. Applying thick layers of liquid water-repellant sealant—polyurethane, resins, silicones, or waxes will seal the ends and keep bamboo dry. Keeping bamboo elevated, touching neither soil nor water, will prolong its usefulness.

- The end cuts of bamboo are also susceptible to powder-post beetle attack if the starchy liquid of a freshly cut culm is not leached out or replaced. Soaking the bamboo with a boron treatment or smoking the stems to cure them will encourage the insects to go elsewhere for their meals.

Facing: The small open-air pavilion on Linda Garland's property is supported by coconut-palm-wood columns on a solid concrete-and-river-stone foundation. Shading the cut stalks from direct sun or rain, the wide-brimmed, layered thatch "straw hat" is built with generous eaves that effectively protect the bamboo construct.

In a mix of traditional and contemporary, this nicely detailed bamboo chair was made by Thomasville Furniture in the 1970s. It spent some thirty years indoors and out-doors. After the sun-bleached chair had been cleaned, repaired, rebuilt, and lovingly restored, many coatings of a beeswax balsam were applied to protect it for its renewed life.

Bamboo is Affordable.

- Living bamboo available at nurseries and at regional bamboo society auctions can be purchased for reasonable prices—a five-gallon container falls in the $25 to $50 range. Large and rare specimens can, however, command a high premium.

- While the initial costs may seem high, once you start planting bamboo, you can transplant rhizomes and quickly increase the size of your harvest—making bamboo a very economical investment.

- Cut-bamboo poles can range in cost from $20 to $35 per piece, and sometimes more, depending on diameter, length, and color.

- Bamboo flooring, ply-bamboo, tambours (bamboo strips spaced close together and attached to a fabric backing), and veneers are priced competitively with hardwoods. For example, bamboo flooring costs between $5 and $7 per square foot. (*See* Sourcebook—Flooring.)

Potted bamboo plants are sheltered in one of the greenhouses at the Bamboo Sourcery nursery in Sebastopol, California.

Bamboo Spirit

The dominant tendencies and character of bamboo define its "spirit."

It is a metaphor for living a strong, healthy life.

The essence of bamboo is represented by its vigor, life energy ("chi"), and zeal, and is embodied in how it grows.

Bamboo remains green throughout the year, representing *endurance*. As a full culm and as a split stalk, bamboo represents *integrity*. Although its vertical fibers are separated by splitting, the thinner strips remain straight and true.

Patience and *resilience* are represented by bamboo's ability to bend under strong wind, rain, and snow—and when the sunshine returns, to once again become upright and tall.

The Ways of Bamboo

Over centuries and generations, there have been grassroots efforts to integrate bamboo's multiplicity of uses in cultures as disparate as those in Japan, Thailand, Indonesia, the Caribbean, Central America, and western North America.

It is glorious to snuggle into the deep, soft, white canvas-covered cushions on the timber-bamboo sofas and side chairs, kick off your sandals, and rest your toes on a bamboo coffee table. Closing your eyes, you enjoy cool breezes. Slowly opening your eyes and looking up, you have a wonderful visual: the ceiling of the small open-air pavilion at Panchoran. The exposed underside of the roof structure has a light-and-dark rhythm of bamboo and coconut-palm wood. Night lighting is powered with wire passing through the hollowed timber bamboo "conduit." Two bamboo-culm incandescent, dimmable downlights give off a soft glow to the bamboo structure, furniture, and furnishings.

Traditional Bamboo Ways

In the Asian countries where tropical species grow, tools and weapons such as beautifully crafted bows and arrows, carved spears, and swords have been fashioned from bamboo. However, bamboo utilization is not limited to the Pacific Rim—the banana republics are now actively involved: Ecuador has hosted an international conference; Costa Ricans are growing their own homes; Colombians are designing earthquake-safe houses for areas devastated by the temblors.

More than three thousand years ago, interest in bamboo traveled from the Far East cultures westward to Europe. After experiencing a long period of favor, bamboo's popularity faltered until the 1300s, when it was reinvigorated with renewed trade activity between the Asian and European markets. Chinese silk traders gave gifts made of bamboo to their wealthy European clients. The Europeans also received presents of living bamboos for planting in their estate gardens. These parks are now amongst the oldest bamboo stands found in Europe. East Indian bamboo furniture, decorative objects, and creative artworks found their way to Europe as well.

Bamboo is still a vibrant presence in Europe today. Although no species are native to the Continent, it is the home of several of the most loved and admired bamboo nurseries and long-established

A stunning example of sensuous, straight stalks shaped and fastened together to form a framework for flowering, climbing plants is found along a footpath at La Bambouseraie nursery in the Cévenne region of France. This tubular bamboo-framed pergola spans across the garden's walkway that is edged with smaller-diameter bamboos joined together to form a railing of simplicity and function.

Roll-up bamboo matchstick shades allow an afternoon siesta to be private and shaded while the Balinese breezes pass through. One can easily appreciate the conscious design using local materials and the indigenous style of the architecture located adjacent to the rice fields. There is most always an altar outside a dwelling—like the one in the foreground—where small offerings are placed at sunrise, noontime, and sunset.

gardens: La Bambouseraie in Prafrance, Anduze, located in the Cévenne region of France; and Wolfgang Ebert's bamboo nursery in Baden-Baden, Germany—Bambus-Centrum Deutschland. Fantastic outdoor bamboo sculptures and bridges are being designed and built in Europe, and structural testing of bamboo varieties is conducted in the laboratory at Einhoven University in the Netherlands.

Traditional Bamboo Buildings

"Pillar, beam, ceiling, floor, walls of woven bamboo covered with clay, roofs from split semicircles facing up and down alternately—rustic or sophisticated, all its architectural uses reveal the beauty of simplicity."

—Austin, Levy, Ueda, *Bamboo*, p. 44.

Far Eastern cultures have been constructing buildings with bamboo for the longest amount of time. The Japanese use bamboo auspiciously in a teahouse or dwelling, where, as a featured support column, it draws attention to its form and beauty in contrast to wooden structural elements. They use it mostly for decoration and ornamentation in reverence of its spiritual qualities.

A two- to four-inch-diameter culm is sometimes used as a gabled-roof rafter in bamboo dwellings found in Southeast Asia, Indonesia, and other Pacific Rim countries. Smaller-diameter bamboo pieces snugged close to each other create a patterned infill between the rafters. These ceiling treatments can be an orthogonal, or angular, design expression. The façade of a residence in Taiwan is built with bamboo stalks spaced closely together and arranged vertically.

A powerful angled series of bamboo culms are sculpted by architect Rocco Yim into a framework reflected in the pool outside the exhibition space at Haus der Kulturen der Welt in Berlin, Germany, October 1999, for their temporary installation "Festival of Visions."

The exterior walls of this Balinese residence are woven with split lengths of bamboo. The colorful and intricate carvings on the door and window shutters are crafted in wood and painted by local artisans. Timber-bamboo full culms support the wide wooden top railing of the covered veranda. Bamboo rafters, beams, and ties hold up the clay-tile roof. At night the matchstick shades become a moveable wall permeable to the evening breezes. The principles of a "good hat" are here—no direct sunlight or rain for the bamboo. Totally the opposite, the tiled outdoor bathroom is completely open to the sky.

The Chinese speak of bamboo as their friend and integrate bamboo in their philosophy and way of being. For them, bamboo has a sacred place in their religious temple structures.

Bamboo poles, woven bamboo mattings, flattened or plaited bamboo panels, and split-bamboo roof shingles are some of the traditional ways bamboo is used in Bali, to create their indigenous built form. Other organic materials—coconut wood, grasses and reeds for roofing thatch, earthen stucco, and stone are used in combination with bamboo. Traditional Balinese bamboo dwellings grouped in family compounds last five to ten years, sometimes longer; eventually the bamboo crumbles, returning its essence to the soil. This impermanence of bamboo is its nature, its *wabi sabi*: ". . . a beauty of things imperfect, impermanent, and incomplete" (Leonard Koren, *Wabi-Sabi*, p . 7).

In Central and South America, builders and designers recognize qualities that make bamboo an ideal building material. Here, bamboo has been cultivated, harvested, and ingeniously employed architecturally to create simple shelters and complex buildings, spiritual retreats and international pavilions. Woven bamboo lattice saturated with a cementitious mixture creates a roof diaphragm that resists shear (uplift from strong winds) and forces from earthquake shocks. On farms and ranches, livestock are restricted by bamboo corrals and cages.

Bamboo is both the internal support and the woven covering for this African hut.

In Africa, an Ethiopian hut is crafted with an underlying bamboo structure covered with a woven bamboo material.

Classical Interior Uses

"The ages have linked it so inseparably with the concept of home itself that bamboo still finds a place, greater or lesser, inside every house."

—Austin, Levy, Ueda, *Bamboo*, p. 44.

Facing: Japanese lacquered panels of this étagère are set into the geometric bamboo frame. It is possible, though not certain, that in the 1800s, English furniture maker W. T. Elmore & Son created this striking Victorian design. Available at Newell Art Galleries, Inc.

The same populations that construct their buildings with bamboo—in Southeast Asia, the Pacific Rim, India, and Africa—also use bamboo in their interiors as walls and ceilings, wall and ceiling finishes, panels, and moveable screens. These interior treatments are made from bamboo matting that is split and flattened; then the nodes are removed and the inside surfaces are scraped and cleaned. The prepared pieces are finally woven together.

Perret &Fils &Vibert, a French furniture company, manufactured this bamboo settee. The influence of Chinese trellis designs is depicted in the styled seat back where the rattan woven crescents are integrated with angled and curved bamboo pieces. Available at Newell Art Galleries, Inc.

Since the Sung Dynasty (ca. 960–1280), Chinese methods of furniture joinery and construction have been adapted and used around the world. By the early nineteenth century, Chinese domestic bamboo furniture designs were still not very sophisticated. They used simple forms and joinery. However, the Chinese refined the art of making bamboo furniture when silk traders introduced the imports to their wealthy European clientele. The Chinese exported bamboo furniture pieces that were elaborately designed with intricate latticework and glossy lacquered surfaces. According to Emily Newman Greenspan in her article *"Bamboozled!"* (*Shop Talk*, November/December 1998), the most important and exposed furniture parts were lacquered, while the less-prominent features were not. In some furniture, Japanese-embossed

leather paper was introduced in places where it was less noticeable. Woven mats made of other grasses were also fashioned into furniture panels.

The furniture crafters made burn marks on the light-colored bamboo to create a richly darkened surface. This tortoiseshell effect—coupled with capping the end-nodes with materials such as metal, ivory, or bone—was very attractive to the European market. The organic design features of the bamboo rhizome were shaped into newel-post caps, finials, drawer pulls, handles, and furniture feet.

Bamboo style began to quickly gain favor with Europe's designers and manufacturers. During the eighteenth century in Victorian England, Thomas Chippendale featured Chinese bamboo motifs in his carved wooden furniture. In the late 1700s, the Prince Regent received a gift of Chinese wallpapers for the Chinese Gallery at the Brighton Pavilion. This helped bamboo win favor in the artistic sensibilities of the country's designers. English cabinetmakers used bamboo in furniture, and they also turned and carved wood with faux-bamboo motifs. (This effect is popular again and is prevalent on metal and wood lamp bases, picture frames, and furniture legs, for example.) The *look* of bamboo interpreted in wood was highly desirable in wet, rainy England, as carved wood lasted much longer than real bamboo in extreme weather. During a period of nearly sixty-five years in the late 1800s and early 1900s, England registered about 150 bamboo furniture manufacturers.

Persian glazed tiles and thin bamboos depicting an Oriental script are features of this Victorian bamboo pedestal. Available at Newell Art Galleries, Inc.

China and the United States created a friendly trade accord in the mid-1780s. At that time, bamboo furniture began to be exported to the American marketplace. About thirty years later, furniture makers in Boston and New York City used maple to make both fancy and common faux-bamboo settees and chairs.

Concurrently, the French exported a different type of bamboo furniture to America. They manufactured pieces that had a heavier look, with ornate decoration and upholstered sections. The bamboo framework was stained in a range of rich colors. Probably the largest quantity of bamboo furniture manufactured in France was by Perret & Fils & Vibert.

Within fifty years, the Chinese began to export fewer bamboo furniture pieces to Europe and the United States because they were reluctant to alter their designs in response to Western demands.

Classical Exterior Uses

Vernacular bamboo dwellings are just one type of traditional structures found in the outdoor environment. When an untreated bamboo structure is exposed to the weather, the color of the outdoor architecture will eventually change—from a gorgeous green when it's first cut, to a golden yellow, and eventually to a bleached, pale tan.

Fences and gates made of bamboo define property boundaries in many different cultures. Japanese fence designs developed during the eighteenth and nineteenth centuries are illustrated in pen-and-ink drawings. Fences expressive of the Japanese aesthetic were integrated into the garden setting of the teahouse and its ritual ceremony.

Tiered, split culms become an elevated water conduit, stretching across the landscape.

As functional sculpture, bridges of bamboo gracefully spanned rivers and gorges. To prevent soil erosion on steep slopes, bamboo retention walls were often dug into hillsides. Aqueducts of bamboo half-cylinders with the nodes removed made functional water conduits.

Garden pergolas and trellises created shady places of retreat and contemplation. A bamboo fountain with its steady gentle flow of water provided a peaceful element in the outdoor space.

Bamboo in Contemporary Architecture

"Tradition only comes truly alive when we feel it from inside, sense the bones beneath the historical expression, and discover relevant contemporary forms for ourselves."

—David Farrelly, *The Book of Bamboo*, p. 108.

In 1998, Colombian architect Simón Vélez asked the elementary school children in his hometown of Manizales how many of them lived in bamboo houses. They lowered their heads, embarrassed. (In Colombia, building with brick, concrete, and steel represents a higher economic status.) Then Simón showed slides and told stories of his own work building with bamboo. After his presentation, the students were asked if they would like to work with Simón and learn how to build with bamboo. They all raised their hands and stood up cheering!

In many parts of the world where it is considered the "poor man's timber," bamboo's abundance and availability as a construction material has given the local people a means to build rudimentary dwellings. Because of this association, the wealthier populations have been reluctant to embrace bamboo in their buildings. Acceptance of this beautiful and relatively inexpensive material by people of financial means as a viable renewable resource is essential for bamboo to gain the respect it deserves.

It is the "bamboo children"—*takenoko*, in Japanese—who will learn about and work to change the attitude towards building with bamboo. It is talented designers and teachers like Simon and his artisan/builder colleague Marcelo Villegas who demonstrate the enormous possibilities of the structural and design elegance of creatively constructing with bamboo.

Because architect Simón Vélez doesn't do structural calculations, Colombian bamboo constructors created the first ZERI pavilion designed by him in his hometown of Manizales so the German engineers could test the structure. Once they approved the bamboo construction, the same workers constructed a second ZERI pavilion in Germany for the Hannover 2000 Expo. This design elevated building with bamboo to a new stature internationally, with a renewed respect for bamboo as a formidable architectural material.

Vélez's beautiful buildings elevate bamboo as a respected material both structurally and aesthetically. He achieves masterful, expansive roof cantilevers that freely span nearly twenty feet. He designs ingenious systems of bamboo trusses and buttressed supports. The resulting structures are awesome to behold and experience.

Simón Vélez designed and directed the construction of the bamboo pavilion for the ZERI (Zero Emissions Research Initiative) organization at the Hannover 2000 Expo in Germany. Before the ZERI pavilion was constructed, he designed and built a full-scale test model in Manizales, Colombia. During the process, he had his builders cut two each of all the pieces. After testing the Colombian structure, German engineers were satisfied with the building's performance and allowed the same pavilion to be built in Hannover. More than twenty containers were loaded with the duplicate pieces cut in Colombia and then shipped to Germany for construction. From May until October 2000, the ZERI Pavilion welcomed thousands of visitors to view the extensive range and diversity of design that bamboo allows. The construction detailing of the bamboo pavilion combined steel and concrete with bamboo rhizomes (underground stems) and culms (upright stalks), which made recycling of the structure by disassembling and reassembling impractical. In January 2001, the pavilion was demolished to clear the Hannover site for another international trade fair.

At Linda Garland's Bali estate, Panchoran, structures are built with bamboo, thatch, coconut palm wood, and some concrete and stone. Garland founded the Environmental Bamboo Foundation and established its office headquarters on the second floor of a bamboo building, distinguished by a set of bamboo stairs that are lashed together with coconut twine and creak a sigh of "welcome" as one ascends.

The Big Living Pavilion includes a bamboo stair-ladder leading to the second-level sitting and dressing room. This three-level bamboo structure, with its broad overhanging eaves and steep thatched roof, is centrally located on the property. It is the main gathering shelter—a place where one can find relief from the intense sun and heavy rains. The pavilion's main structure has been expanded to include two wings and a large, raised, stone deck.

Guest cottages called "baskets" are built with bamboo roof rafters, woven-bamboo walls, and flattened-bamboo flooring. Hanging outside each basket's entry door is a bamboo raincoat—a woven-bamboo shell to cover one's head and back while venturing outside

Above: The creaking of a bamboo stair-ladder tied together with Balinesian tali (coconut twine) announces comings and goings. The broad thatched roof of the Big Living Pavilion at Panchoran acts like an umbrella, protecting the stair, bamboo roof structure, coconut-palm columns, and all the furnishings.
Below: The woven-bamboo walls at Linda Garland's "Basket" guest house invite one to pause and appreciate the elegance in this architectural design and execution. With a closer look, one discovers a portable "basket"—a woven raincoat resting on a hook just to the side of the door. This shell is for wearing during torrential rains and tapering showers.
Facing: Warm temperatures, blue sky, and palm trees. Take some time and be comforted in Linda Garland's tropical Bali environment. Her timber bamboo lounge chairs with their deep canvas-cushioned seat and back, plus the coffee table, are protected under the bamboo roof-framed pavilion.

An example of the bamboo housing built for the National Bamboo Housing Project in Costa Rica was constructed from bamboo grown for this specific purpose—a true practice of growing your own housing. Full culms were used for columns; bamboo splits were assembled into the roof trusses. Smaller-diameter bamboos make breathable wall panels.

Colombian architect Oscar Hidalgo directed the construction of this *bahareque* wall mock-up at the Bali Bamboo Festival. Full bamboo culms are used for vertical-support framing "studs." Split bamboo slats are the horizontal lathing covered with a gridded metal screen. The final layers are cement-based stucco.

during a heavy tropical rainstorm. Inside all of the bamboo buildings at Panchoran, classic Bali bamboo architectural décor is made contemporary with Linda's original timber-bamboo furniture designs. The seats and backs of the furniture have thick, sumptuous cushions covered with heavyweight, white cotton woven fabrics that are both elegant and comfortable.

In Costa Rica, the National Bamboo Housing Project, which, unfortunately, is no longer operational, grew, harvested, treated, and cured their own bamboo construction material—a very real example of "growing your own house." Bamboo poles were used as posts and formed a building structural system together with split bamboo that was joined to create triangulated roof trusses. A woven-bamboo lattice wraps the structural skeleton, which is then covered with cement mortar.

A similar technique, called *bahareque*, is used in Colombia. Bamboo poles are the building's framework—similar to a wood stud wall. The bamboo culms are then covered with a split and flattened bamboo lath or expanded metal mesh lath. The final layer is a troweled-on plaster finish that hides the bamboo internal structure and gives strength to the wall. The stucco finish is a symbol of wealth. In both Costa Rica and Colombia, this type of construction has successfully withstood seismic shakers.

After the Colombian earthquake in January 1999, almost all of the structures that had been built with something other than bamboo—for instance, brick or concrete—collapsed. Subsequently, Simón Vélez designed a bamboo housing prototype that was used to speedily rebuild the region. Because "bamboo bounces," according to Linda Garland, and "bamboo houses dance along to the tunes of the earth" (Garland, quoted in *Grow Your Own House*, p. 202), building with bamboo is a sensible and appropriate material for constructing earthquake-safe structures.

Australian nurseryman Dunford Dart led a team of volunteers at the Bali Bamboo Festival who built a geodesic structure using whole bamboo culms with metal connectors as a demonstration prototype. The construction used similar synergistic design principles as the tensegrity structures of North American inventive engineer R. Buckminster Fuller.

Guadua bamboo rafters frame the roof of a Colombian residence. A deep saturation of colors is achieved with pigments applied to the exposed concrete underside of the roof diaphragm.

With a team of helpers at the Bali Bamboo Festival, Australian bamboo nurseryman Durnford Dart constructed this geodesic-structure prototype for an emergency shelter. Full-timber bamboo culms are joined together with a metal "star plate" connector normally used with wood lengths—adapted to bamboo.

After a twilight sleep of more than fifty years, bamboo's culture and uses are reawakening in the West. In addition to horticultural research, there have been research activities concerning the construction applications of bamboo. David Farrelly, in *The Book of Bamboo*, tells us that fifty years ago, at Clemson University's engineering department, they were experimenting with bamboo as concrete reinforcement. He also refers to West Coast bamboo architect Jim Orjala, who expanded the use of bamboo lattice weaving to provide reinforcement for a ferro-cement construction in a domed vault. This thin layer of composite materials creates an efficient structural shape that spreads out the stresses and minimizes bending.

Not having plentiful supplies of indigenous timber bamboo in North America has limited its use as a building material. The lack of recognized standards for building with bamboo has also impacted not building with bamboo in North America.

Stick-built construction has been the leading method of residential construction in North America because of plentiful wood forests, industrialized millworks, and lumberyard distribution. Unlike the Asian populations, North Americans don't depend on bamboo for shelter. As a result, interest in bamboo as a building material has only recently been considered a viable alternative to old-growth forests.

Bamboo construction in the United States is just beginning to garner approval from some local building departments. In Maui, Hawaii, Eco Architects' principal architect, David Sands, has worked in partnership with Bamboo Hardwoods of Seattle, Washington, and with Maui-based consultant and construction manager Jeffree Trudeau to develop some of the first permitted bamboo structures. They received permission to build a ferro-cement house using bamboo forms that remained in place. However, most building codes in the U.S. have yet to incorporate building standards for bamboo, which has delayed recognition of building with bamboo in mainstream construction.

A core group of engineers, architects, and building officials from around the world are working to create a prescriptive code for building with bamboo. They hope that universally applied knowledge published in the form of an International Building Code will impact building conditions and the

The bamboo-framed roof overhang of this Bamboo Technologies dwelling is laced with a rhizome bracket detail that takes advantage of the natural bent and visually interesting organic structure of the underground stem of the bamboo.

approval process for such alternative structures. Most recently, engineering tests that can be quantified for specific species are being performed at Washington State University in Pullman. These types of calculations will, hopefully, provide data to establish adequate structural guidelines for building with bamboo. The physical properties of bamboo identify it as an inherently high-tech material that, up until recently, has mostly been used in low-tech applications.

EcoArchitects and Bamboo Hardwoods have contracted with three

U.S. structural testing labs for evaluating the bamboo used in two of their prototypes. These designers and constructors recognize that there is tremendous potential for bamboo cultivation in Hawaii, and seek to develop a market for the harvest. This could lead to the first bamboo timber yard, with species identification, grading, and structural testing

results to guide the designs for bamboo building applications. The attitude of living lightly on the planet has encouraged builders and consumers to adapt alternative construction techniques, including straw bale, rammed earth, and reclaimed timber. In some straw-bale buildings, bamboo poles are used effectively as roof trusses and reinforcement.

The organic form of a retreat hermitage in northern California is built with straw bales, cob, Douglas-fir wattle and daub, and bamboo roof trusses. Architect Darrel DeBoer designed the bamboo roof construction using two species: *Phyllostachys nigra* 'Henon' and *Dendrocalamus strictus.* Exterior ornamentation of several angled bamboo poles adds a textural layer to the earthen-plaster wall surface. Woven bamboo matting is applied to the interior ceilings.

Bamboo is an excellent choice for making a temporary booth, or sukkah, for the ancient annual Jewish harvest festival of thanksgiving and renewal. A sukkah's requirements are that the structure must be open to the sky, it must have at least three walls, and the roof cannot attach directly to the walls. Bamboo branches and leaves can be used for the roofing, which must be a production of the earth. The sukkah walls can be made of woven bamboo, split and flattened bamboo, bamboo matchstick shades, or a natural fabric imprinted or embroidered with a bamboo motif.

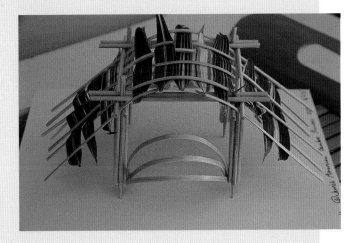

The author built a scale model from bamboo skewers and leaves for the Sukkah Project art installation at the Santa Barbara Bronfman Family Jewish Community Center and wrote the following description:

Bamboo Sukkah

Bamboo is a versatile grass that is
    beautiful, strong, flexible, renewable,
    sustainable, workable, and affordable.
Bamboo was chosen to craft this model as a
    symbol of the harvest festival—
    the living bamboo is harvested and
    used throughout—
    as the vertical supports, the beams,
    the splayed walls, the rafters, and
    the roofing.
As in a Japanese teahouse, you must bend to
    enter, an act which humbles the visitor
    while making the transition into the space.
The Japanese concept of *wabi sabi* is also expressed
    in the structure—imperfect, impermanent,
    and incomplete.

When a very slow, subtle, and deliberate drip of water releases from this spout at the Japanese Garden in Portland, Oregon, a gentle ripple expands outward to the edges of the diamond-shaped cutout in the square stone basin.

This is the type of landscape element one would be pleased to encounter as an oasis under a shaded canopy of bamboo, where mottled light splashes across the fountain's surface.

Backyard Bamboo Creations

Cut bamboo culms combine to create garden elements—benches, bridges, fences, and gates. Straight shafts of this sensuous stalk can be shaped into shade structures, trellises, and pergolas that provide weather protection and a framework for growing grapes and flowering vines.

While students attend training at a southern California yoga educational center, they stay in canvas yurts and simple wood cabins. Adjacent to these structures is a "Room with a View"—a unisex, modern-plumbed outhouse with a view of the canyon and the ocean from the throne. Bamboo, reed, and wood together create a pleasing geometry in a Zen-inspired design for the side panels of the bathroom house.

One way to create a cool and calming effect outdoors is to introduce a bamboo fountain in the garden sanctuary. A trickle of water flowing or dripping from a bamboo spout into a contained pool or a flowing Rubicon creates a peaceful sound and is visually attractive.

Small, curved splits of bamboo can be put into the ground to mark the edge of a planting bed or garden walkway.

Beverly Messenger designed an unusual "Room with a View," built of wood, bamboo, reed, and copper. A delightful surprise awaits the user—an ocean and canyon view.

Very thin and flexible bamboo is bent into curves and grounded between stones, defining the bounds of a garden pathway.

Advocates for Bamboo

For many years, corrugated aluminum panels were identified as a building material associated with basic shelters found in rural parts of North America. Only when architects, designers, builders, and clients—who can afford the cost premiums that initially go along with alternative and innovative ways of doing something—began using the rippled aluminum panels in high-tech, postmodern, deconstructionist, and contemporary design, did the perceptions of the material's image change. A mundane, conventional construction material gained a new respect. Attitudes change more easily when there's a boost from people with influence, the trendsetters, and those on the edge who push the envelope and expand the possibilities.

At the World Bamboo Congress in Bali, two "Designers for the Environment" forums brought architects, builders, artists, and businesspeople together. They shared ideas about building with bamboo, bamboo in arts and crafts, and bamboo's role in eco-environmental awareness. Each participant became an advocate for the use and planting of this great grass. Professional architects and designers who were there as students, learning about the possibilities of creating bamboo architecture, returned to their homelands and began building with bamboo. They became activists as educators teaching about bamboo.

The Sourcebook provides more information about specific bamboo advocates.

The Bamboo Fencer constructed this sturdy timber-bamboo fence. Vertical pieces about three feet tall and spaced about a foot apart are tied along the lower portion by two split bamboo lengths on either side. A pyramidal stacking arrangement at the top of the verticals forms a cap and top rail that covers the culms' ends and provides weather protection.

Contemporary Bamboo Arts and Crafts

Working with bamboo in their own way—as medium or motif—artists and craftspeople are playing a role in advancing bamboo in popular culture. Their materials vary from harvested bamboo to watercolor, acrylic, metal, stone, and concrete. And they use bamboo wholly alone, split or woven.

Two artists who interpret the powerful spirit of bamboo through watercolor are Bay Area architect and artist Shari Arai DeBoer and southern California graphic artist Gary Chafe. DeBoer traded her straightedge and triangles for a bamboo brush. Her bamboo sensibility is interwoven with her Japanese heritage and is depicted in her descriptive paintings. For Shari, "A grove of bamboo creates a peaceful, reflective place to be. In my paintings, I try to convey this serenity."

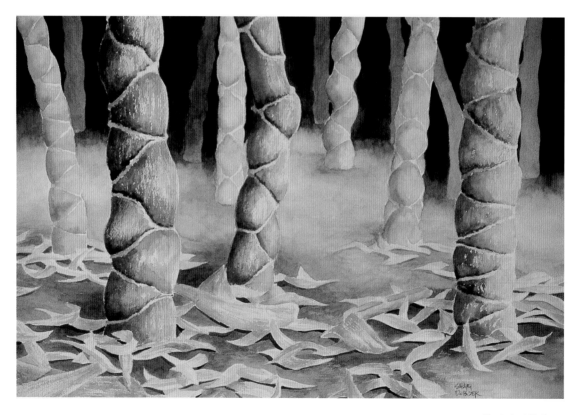

Shari Arai DeBoer
Tortoiseshell Grove, 1999, 15" x 22"

Gary Chafe is a southern California graphic artist who paints Japanese *sumi-e* watercolors of bamboo. "Each brush has its own facets as the ink thickens and thins on the arborings and yielding paper in an ancient rhythm," says Chafe.

Gary Chafe
Bamboo sumi-e
watercolor, 30" x 20"

Much bolder and more intense colors of bamboo weavings with realistic flowers are the palette of a southern California painter in oil and acrylic, Dorothy Churchill-Johnson, whose artworks would fit comfortably in a tropical decor. "Bamboo chainlink fence, Beyond that the stars even—Promise of freedom," says Dorothy Churchill-Johnson.

Dorothy Churchill-Johnson
Beyond that the Stars Even—Promise of Freedom,
pen and ink/acrylics, 30" x 50"

Nancy Moore Bess, maker of exquisite baskets, creates her vessels in her Amherst, Massachusetts, studio. She translates a "layering of two cultures" with plaited bamboo representing Japan and its basketry with twined, waxed cord that reflects Bess's own culture.

Says Bess of her work, "Bamboo is often the direct link between nature and my own creativity—the connection between the great outdoors, which is awe-inspiring, and one's inner spirit."

Nancy Moore Bess
Jar from Kawagoe to New York,
Japanese bamboo, waxed cord, old Japanese *netsuke,* 3 1/2" x 5"

Other bamboo artists work with the third dimension, making sculptures of bamboo suited for indoor spaces. Calvin Hashimoto, a Hawaiian sculptor, crafts architectonic creations from bamboo that either hang on the wall or are freestanding. He discovered bamboo groves where he experienced "a serenity and beauty . . . that transported me into a spiritual place of my own being." Through research and trial and error, he has come to know the "eccentricities of this exquisite material and has refined his "own methods of fashioning it into works of art. The difficult task I endeavor to accomplish, is to incorporate some of the aspects of serenity, beauty, and spirituality of a bamboo forest into my artwork."

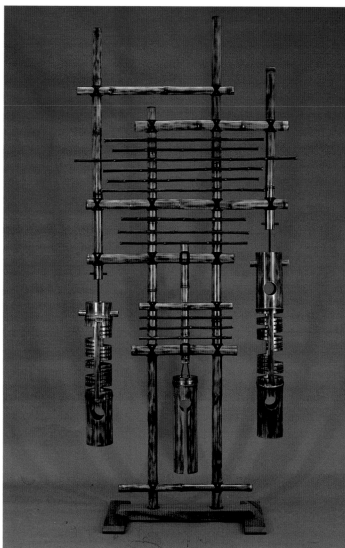

Calvin Hashimoto
Tubular, bamboo and koa wood,
42" x 94" x 5"

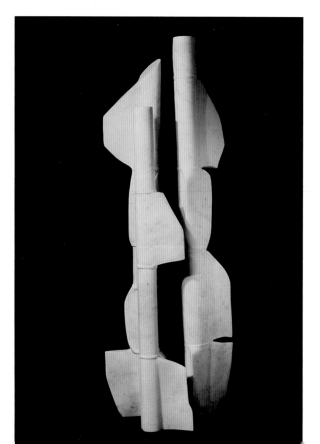

Bamboo is sometimes the chosen motif for sculptors working in other materials. Southern California marble artist Jill Vander Hoof has carved a pivoting sculpture of a bamboo stalk with culm sheaths intact. "In stone I feel and see the fragile grace and tenacious strength of bamboo," she says.

Jill Vander Hoof
Standing Bamboo, carrara marble, 52" x 16" x 13"

An Arizona metalworker, Hazel Colditz, influenced by her Japanese mother and German father, welds stainless-steel tubes into bamboo sculptures that attract attention and endure either in the home or outside in the garden. "The dichotomy, my inner sanctuary, is strong like bamboo," says Colditz.

Hazel Colditz
Untitled, stainless steel

A talented young sculptor, Charissa Brock combines bamboo with other materials. She writes about her relationship to her art and to bamboo: "When working with bamboo I listen to the ways it wants to move, break, and bend. I use its subtleties as a secret language from which to create form, exploring the tension between abstraction and utility."

The works of these and many other bamboo artists complement just about any part of a home environment. Just imagine the possibilities . . .

Charissa Brock
Bamboo, wax linen thread, rock from New Mexico, 5"x 13" x 4"

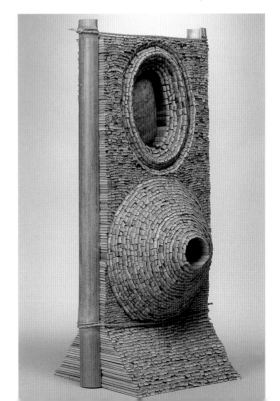

73

Bamboo Inside

Adopting bamboo as a material of choice for your home says something about you and your lifestyle. Whether you envision something exotic or traditional, bamboo can fit comfortably into your design scheme.

Here are some concepts and possibilities that will enable you to live comfortably with bamboo indoors. Options for floors, walls, windows, and ceilings are detailed, with creative ideas for décor in every room of the house.

Bamboo furnishings (lamp pole, coffee table, end tables, plant stand, window shades) and accessories (candlesticks, cases, baskets, and valise, among others) add the richness of natural materials to a traditionally designed and well-balanced living room.

Bamboo devotee Beverly Messenger designed her canyon-home living room with imported Balinese bamboo furniture: a timber-bamboo sofa, side chair, and coffee table. The furnishings and functional accessories include free-standing room-dividing screens, a globe shade made of bamboo and rice paper, a lantern, and a woven bamboo ball. Covering the floor, a woven-grass mat and Oriental rug add complementary texture, color, and warmth.

Below: The meditation room designed by Tania Knox of TK Designs has precious bamboo antiques on the low, wood-topped table—a book fashioned from split bamboo strips tied together with silk thread, a pair of carefully stacked woven-bamboo cases, and a finely carved bamboo-culm-lidded container. An Oriental tri-panel screen with a brushwork painting (likely painted with a bamboo brush) depicts growing bamboo in the landscape. Complementing the bamboo and wood décor is a woven-reed-mat floor covering. Mexican weeping bamboo (*Otatea acuminata aztecorum*) is planted in the garden. The effect is a harmonious bamboo spirit both inside and outside.

Facing, below: With training in architecture in his native Philippines and interior design in New York City, Antonio "Budji" Layug designs furniture crafted from organic materials indigenous to the Philippines and incorporating traditional techniques. He creates timeless environments with a "thoroughly post-colonial" and freshly modern interpretation of furniture. An eclectic mix of traditional and modern-design furniture holistically relate to one another, indoors and outdoors. He brings the outdoors to live inside.

Budji has designed a stone top for a sophisticated and elegant giant-timber-bamboo table base. An assemblage of cut culms is interlocked like fingers clasped together in prayer. The spirit of the piece also recalls a clumping bamboo's natural growth in a grove. In such a stand, bamboo would benefit greatly from a thinning of culms, for when they grow this close together, damage to the culm's surface is likely to mar its beauty. In this case, by bringing the outdoors in, Budji has preserved the beauty of the bamboo in its transformed state.

A contemporary wooden parsons bench with both the seat and back insets made of crushed bamboo panels is available from Pier 1 Imports.

Facing: A South Seas island ambiance of heavenly proportions created by interior designer Corinna Gordon places a Linda Garland–designed giant-timber-bamboo bed on a raised platform with a split bamboo riser frontispiece as the main focal point. It is anchored with wood corner columns and a log-frame canopy softened by cinched scrim draperies. Parts of the wall covering are woven bamboo and others are mats from Kalimantan, made of bamboo strips sewn together. The floor is covered with this same matting.

In a contemporary living room setting, applied bamboo splits line the bottoms of the chairs, blending with the woven fiber of the club chairs. Representing the Arts & Crafts tenets of craftsmanship, these nature-based materials merge the indoors with the outdoors.

Some words about *style*. We develop a style as we make choices for our lives—lifestyle. In the art of designing living spaces, your personal style reflects who you are and how you live. How can bamboo participate in your chosen style? By designing with bamboo furniture and furnishings, you can create a tropical, classical, Zen, or contemporary modern environment. A bamboo furniture selection that includes a giant-timber bamboo sofa, side chairs, and a coffee table can become the dominant furnishings for a great room for the family. Or you can mix antique bamboo pieces with Stickley craftsman furnishings or modern Mies van der Rohe. Be inspired by the images in these pages and then design your own solutions with creativity and imagination.

A Pacific Island bedroom décor designed by Korpinen & Erickson includes the tropical-vegetation-printed bedspread, pillow, and seat cushion on the rattan desk chair. The rattan desk is accessorized with two vases of giant-timber bamboo culms. Above the desk, the coconut palms depicted on the framed canvas relate directly to the furniture made of rattan (a palm).

The primary furniture pieces—the four-poster bed and armoire—are both contemporary timber-bamboo-framed elements with a tapered design. The unique bamboo-motif handles on the armoire are crafted from metal. Two side tables next to the bed are bamboo and rattan. The combination of Oriental area rugs, an upholstered armchair, a woven-grass lounge chair, wood coffee table, and glass-topped table base fits well with the bamboo-and-rattan furniture ensemble.

A contemporary wall sculpture commissioned of Calvin Hashimoto was made specifically for this location. Called *Paean O Hawaii (Song of Hawaii)*, it is the artist's interpretation of a story about the different cultures that constitute a rich and complex Hawaiian society. The layering of the architecture with the artwork integrates the stone surface of the fireplace wall with the bamboo, reeds, and pine branches. Above the fireplace, the coffered ceiling and skylight are trimmed with both half-round and full-diameter bamboo culms that have been heat-treated to achieve a dark chocolate color. The bars at the top of the piece and the fireplace surround are hammered and patinaed copper.

A bamboo Zen ambiance in a contemporary setting is a wonderful and unexpected surprise in this modest mobile home. A selective set of unique bamboo antiques collected by the designer, Tania Knox, is artistically arranged and tastefully displayed. A bamboo version of Mies van der Rohe's Pavilion Barcelona chair sits comfortably alongside the original chrome-steel and leather design.

Bamboo covers the floor throughout this contemporary oceanfront condominium designed by interior designer Barbara Farish in a "Hawaiian island upscale rental" style. Philippines-imported timber bamboo is fashioned into a sofa, side armchairs, ottoman, étagère, and coffee table. Comfy cotton canvas cushions and pillows soften the bamboo seating. The bamboo furniture is complemented by a pair of woven-sea grass chairs. A coiled bamboo bowl made in Vietnam adds to the coffee table décor. The end-table lamp shaft is crafted in metal with a bamboo motif.

On the Floor

In the Pacific Rim, bamboo has been underfoot for generations. For example, woven mats and split strips cover bare dirt and subfloors in Bali. Unfortunately, both of these coverings result in an uneven walking surface. Fortunately, bamboo is available today in planks—just like hardwood flooring and at a comparable price.

Environmental considerations of sustainability favor bamboo over hardwood. In China, for instance, the government regulates the bamboo harvest. Only culms at least three years old may be cut. The stalks are marked and dated to keep track of their ages. When the stalk is cut, it is not necessary to replant, as bamboo takes care of itself by sending up new shoots each spring. The time factor in replenishing a bamboo harvest is one-tenth that of a hardwood forest.

How do you get flat planks from round bamboo? Daniel Smith, co-founder of the bamboo manufacturing company Smith & Fong-Plyboo, headquartered in San Francisco with manufacturing facilities in China, explains that Chinese farmers have one- to two-acre plots where bamboo is harvested every other year. Lengths of twelve to fourteen feet are preferred because they have the most uniformity in diameter. The process for making laminated flooring starts with splitting four- to six-inch-diameter culms into strips about an inch or so wide. Next, the cut strips are treated by placing them in a solution of boric acid and lime, and then boiling them. This method reduces the starch content in the strips, deterring insects. The nontoxic boric acid that remains in the strips acts as an insect repellent.

The strips are dried either in kilns or naturally in the air. Both of these methods maintain the natural, light golden-yellow color. But the strips turn amber throughout when they are subjected to a special process that includes pressure-cooking.

Flat-grain laminated bamboo flooring
maintains uninterrupted visual continuity
from the kitchen to the dining area.

At William Laman's, split-slatted mats are rolled and displayed in a large woven bamboo basket. The mats can be used on a floor, wall, or ceiling surface to add a layer of natural texture.

In this newly constructed southern California hillside home, prefinished bamboo flooring on the grand staircase's curving treads and risers leads to the second-floor level. The black iron railing spirals up in striking contrast to the golden-toned bamboo. A living black bamboo (*Phyllostachys nigra*) fills the stairwell volume. Home designed by architect Robert Peale Mehl.

Facing: Plyboo, rather than a maple or ash hardwood, is the dominant interior surface material throughout Sushi Yasuda, a NYC Japanese restaurant. The laminated bamboo millwork, seen here at a corner of the maître d' station, is a complementary contrast in color and coolness with the bluestone tile flooring below.

The cut, treated, and dried strips are then milled to get a uniform measurement of three-fourths inch wide by one-fourth inch thick. Then, four strips are laminated together on the flat, and two layers are glued on top of each other. The edges of each plank are milled on all four sides with a tongue or a groove. In the end, the floor strips measure three inches wide by one-half inch thick by six feet long.

Bamboo laminate flooring is a stable material that experiences minimal impact from environmental extremes of humidity and dryness; the expansion and contraction of the flooring is less than half as much as red oak. Bamboo has a similar hardness factor as maple and oak (see p. 32).

Bamboo flooring is available prefinished or unfinished. Prefinished boards often have a slight beveled edge and polyurethane or aluminum oxide coating. Unfinished planks are sanded and ready to receive finished matte or glossy coatings in place. Installation of bamboo flooring uses the same tools and techniques as hardwood floor installation, including adhesives—preferably nontoxic—in glue-down situations on a wood, concrete, or other subflooring. If you choose to finish the bamboo floorboards in situ, this would be the

An edge detail with bamboo stair treads, bamboo baseboard, and wood risers connects two floor levels where a mix of different types of bamboo flooring includes flat and vertically laminated planks in natural and amber finishes.

Plyboo flooring is featured throughout this living space, where the interior design décor includes antique Asian chests, wall hangings, an étagère, and an antique bamboo end table and side chair. The natural bamboo floor material is a compatible selection to enhance the Oriental furniture and furnishings. Richard Gervais Collection.

opportunity to give the newly installed floor a really good *coat*. Check first with the flooring manufacturer for their recommendations, but if you put a few extra layers of protection on the bamboo—maybe three to six coatings—the bamboo surface will remain unworn for much longer.

In either case, upkeep is essential: sweeping or vacuuming, cleaning with a Murphy's Oil–type soap, and reapplying protective coatings as needed. Apply furniture protectors (soft felt glides) to the bottoms of furnishings to ensure your bamboo floor will wear better.

To further protect your floor, do your best to create a transition zone between the outside world and your living space: use a woven-grass or recycled-tire doormat, or define an area where everyone removes their shoes so that dirt and debris won't be carried inside.

Several new bamboo flooring products have just entered the market: a milled flooring material—an alternative to oriented strand board (OSB)—is made from bamboo scrap pieces called BOSB (bamboo-oriented strand board); and a "floating bamboo floor," a prefinished, thin veneer of bamboo over a compressed fiberboard substrate (MDF, or medium-density fiberboard), can be used instead of a Pergo- or IKEA-type flooring.

Baseboards, vent covers, stair nosings, thresholds and the like are also made from bamboo.

Up the Wall

The more traditional woven-bamboo panels compose the breathable walls of many structures in tropical zones, where the weather is conducive to these thin panels, and allow air movement and trade winds to pass through. In the cooler and varied temperate climates, woven bamboo panels are applied as a wall finish. The three-dimensional texture and pattern make an attractive tapestry backdrop in many environments, from Arts & Crafts to postmodern contemporary.

A wall treatment using smoothly finished, flat bamboo multi-ply panels is a "greener" alternative to plywood. The sheets of the ply-bamboo panels are laminated and glued similarly to the flooring, but are manufactured and finished without milled edges. Creative designers are using ply-bamboo as finished wall surfaces, cabinetry, and display shelving.

Abby Bussel wrote about the Japanese restaurant Sushi Yasuda in New York City that uses bamboo on *all* its surfaces—the floor, walls, and ceiling. This "monochromatic stage for the main event at Sushi Yasuda" is an attention-getter.* Bamboo was the material of choice by the owner and architect "because of its fresh, pure look and feel." On two of the walls, architect Yoshinari Matsuyama arranged the Plyboo panels in an interlocking pattern. On all the other

Corinna Gordon designed the interiors of this South Pacific island home, where woven bamboo imported from Thailand covers the walls. The angled closets—top and sides—are designed to both minimize dust and make it difficult for tropical bugs to hide. The cabinet is made of split and full bamboo culms. Two accessories, the antique Chinese coolie hat and the bamboo suitcase nestled under the cabinet, are both woven from thin splits of bamboo. The textured ceiling woven matting is also made of bamboo. Bamboo strips that are sewn together create the floor mat.

*"Bamboo Box," *Interior Design* magazine, June 2001, p. 171.

Facing: The basic basket-weave pattern of Plyboo flooring sections presents a textured relief in the "Bamboo Cube" at Sushi Yasuda, a New York City Japanese restaurant. The sushi bar top and serving counter as well as the mill-work base are all created from laminated bamboo planking. The ceiling surface and lighting soffits are also covered in multi-ply bamboo.

The three plots of grass in the window display subtly foreshadow the use of the giant grass within. Looking into the very modern bamboo cube of Sushi Yasuda, one sees all the exposed interior surfaces covered with multi-ply bamboo flooring and panels. The tabletops are made of unfinished laminated bamboo. Architect Yoshinari Matsuyama, of Matsuyama International, wanted the patrons to be able to tactilely experience the bamboo. (When the tight grain of the bamboo withstood several days of a soy sauce puddle, the owner was convinced to allow the untreated surface.)* While the bamboo flooring is laid conventionally, some of the walls are designed in a tapestry of interlocking bamboo panels. This sophisticated Zen design relief, along with the carved niches displaying minimalist flower and vase arrangements, break up the potential monotony of a singular material.

*"Bamboo Box," *Interior Design* magazine, June 2001, p. 171.

walls—except the maître d' station, where he used a material of contrasting color and temperature—he applied the bamboo tongue-and-groove planks as you would on a floor. The effect is cool and calming. This bamboo cube is distinctively modern and definitely pushes the envelope. Other multi-ply-bamboo applications are used for cabinets, displays, and fixtures.

Facing: The crushed-bamboo folding screen available from Pier I Imports adds dimension and acts as a textured backdrop in this contemporary living space that includes an Oriental rug, upholstered sofa, and woven-grass baskets. Interiors designed with an Asian influence often include complementary pieces of bamboo blended with fabrics and carpets that all together create a pleasing "bamboo style."

Off the Wall

A wood-and-rice paper shoji screen acts as a portable partition dividing the eating zone from the living zone. A small lantern rests on a bamboo place mat at the center of the dining table. Matchstick bamboo shades hung on the wall provide a textured backdrop for the framed pictures. The comfortable dining chairs, with sloped backs made of woven bamboo panels within orthogonal timber-bamboo frames, are imported from Bali. Room design by Beverly Messenger.

From the real to the faux, from the split to the processed, there's a considerable range of choices for bamboo wall coverings. Freestanding bamboo screens are a contemporary design option that can soften a transitional area of a room, diffuse harsh sunlight, or provide privacy. The screens can be made of woven, split, or plaited material. Classic Balinese woven bamboo screens or a sliding panel shoji screen made of bamboo and rice paper can separate interior spaces from one another. The translucence of the screen allows a soft light to filter through it. Shoji screens can also subtly separate the inside space from an outside garden.

A screen with a bamboo framework and its fabric complement each other in creating a visual *yin-yang*. The hard, structural bamboo is the *yang*, or "male" frame; the soft textile that fills the panel's void and defines the screen is the *yin*, or "female" energy. Other design possibilities could feature a natural cloth with a printed bamboo motif combined with a black bamboo structural frame, or bamboo matting as a textured, patterned infill panel.

Bamboo for the Window

Smith + Noble takes orders for these bamboo matchstick window coverings, where both the valance and blinds are edged in a katsura-red fabric. This pair of windows was newly constructed as part of a remodel designed by the author where a small balcony was enclosed and transformed into an artist's studio.

Facing: As comfortable in a city apartment as in an island retreat, bamboo proves here that it is suited to all styles of décor. Interior decorator Ann James has a fabulous flair for designing with bamboo in a sophisticated style. In her dining room niche, the sun is filtered by matchstick bamboo shades. An antique bamboo trunk snugs under the wooden buffet table. An intricately detailed Victorian bamboo armchair sits at an angle, breaking up the linearity of the space. A pair of lamp bases designed in ceramic has a bamboo motif. A wide-leafed succulent agave in a boat-shaped woven-grass basket sits in the company of a cross-legged monkey. This modern setting pleasantly succeeds in mixing bamboo and complementary woven grasses in several varieties—furniture, furnishings, and functional objects—with an oak floor, smooth plaster walls, and a hardwood table.

Varying degrees of solar control and privacy for windows can be accomplished with shades made of bamboo matchsticks, bamboo strips, plaited bamboo, or rice paper combined with a bamboo matchstick or strip framework. Split bamboo and rice paper panels, cleverly used as interior window shutters, give a wall texture and dimension.

One can see pretty readily through bamboo matchsticks. If you like morning sun, then a bamboo matchstick shade covering an east-facing window will allow the first filtered light to penetrate the room. Bamboo strips or plaits will increase the degree of privacy. Adding a dense, dark fabric backing to the shade will do the most to increase the light-blocking factor.

A bamboo curtain rod with a hanging natural-material drape is another nice *yin-yang* window-covering solution, easily accomplished and adapted to many styles, and one that is particularly suited to sliding glass doors, which look softer with a fabric curtain hanging over a bamboo pole.

On the Ceiling

If your taste is for familiar tropical décor, there is an architectural design opportunity using bamboo infill between exposed roof rafters.

In some Balinese and Colombian structures, the finished ceiling is the bottommost layer of the roof composition. Thin-diameter bamboos, *chusqueas* for one, are a good choice for a ceiling finish, and are applied to the interior of the structure where the bamboo pieces span between the exposed beams or rafters. This design solution is just beginning to be adapted in American interiors in treatments similar to southwestern *viga* and *latilla* styles.

Other ideas for using bamboo on the ceiling:

- Fasten woven matting directly to a ceiling for texture and definition.
- Attach bamboo tongue-and-groove flooring to a ceiling between exposed rafters or beams.
- Apply laminated flooring directly to a sloped or flat ceiling.
- Design a barrel-vaulted or domed ceiling and apply a tambour finish (bamboo strips glued to a fabric backing) that conforms to the contours.

Facing: An original-design bamboo chandelier by Jo Scheer is suspended from the cathedral ceiling in this home-away-from-home—a Caribbean "Island Ambiance" available for vacation stays (see Sourcebook). A high-rising four-poster canopy bed with a mosquito netting scrim is crafted from timber bamboo. Next to the bed, a bamboo dresser constructed of bamboo panels and built with a tilt-out drawer anchors that part of the multifunctional space. Scheer crafted the bamboo torchiere floor lamp that emits a soft ambient uplight.

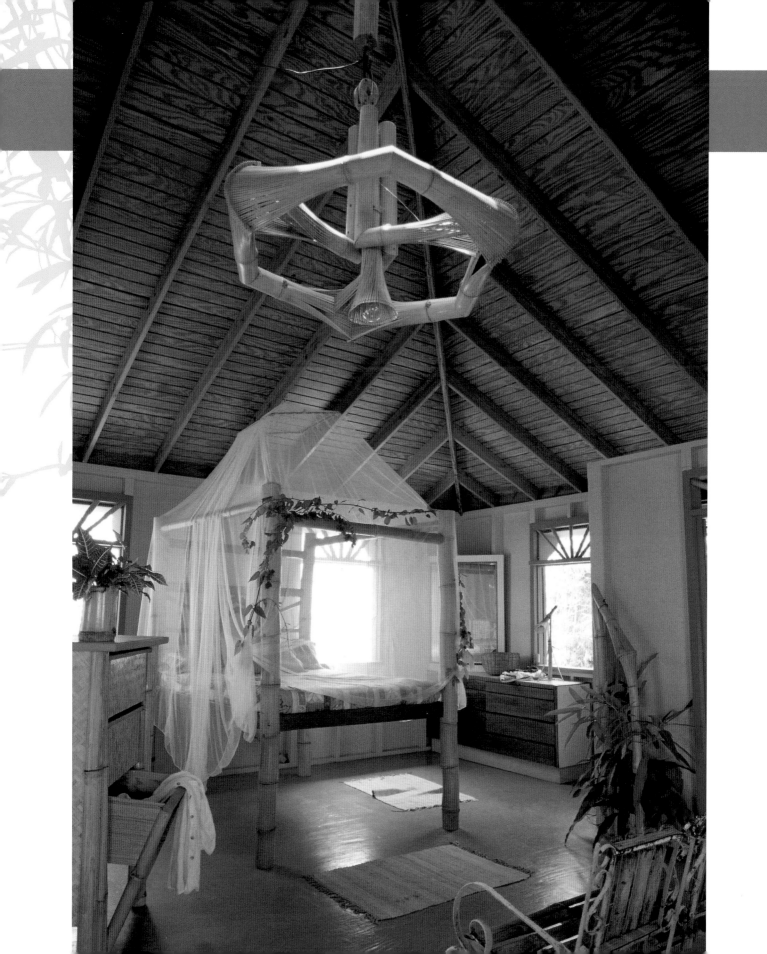

Bamboo in Kitchen, Dining, and Living Spaces

In many contemporary living spaces, rooms are often combined so that one flows into the next and each activity area is defined by furnishings and finishes. At a hilltop home, an edgy residential remodel has one climbing the "stairway to heaven" (words are stenciled on the rough treads) and landing on a natural, prefinished Plyboo floor that covers more than six hundred square feet in the kitchen, dining, and living areas. The floor-vent covers are milled from bamboo and sit about a quarter of an inch above the floor plane.

Two "green" design firms in Santa Barbara, California—Blackbird Architects and Van Atta Associates-Landscape Architecture, share this small, efficient kitchen where the cabinetry is crafted from Smith & Fong Plyboo. An exposed concrete block wall and smooth gypsum wallboard span between the bamboo millwork of the upper cabinets and the stone countertop. The floor is a beeswax-finished concrete. The contemporary design is both practical and visually appealing. Similar built-in bamboo cabinetry is designed for the unisex bathroom across the entry hall.

Facing: It took some time, and architect Gale Beth Goldberg was patient. Penny Cortright, a talented artist who commissioned her to redesign and remodel this home, finally chose prefinished Smith & Fong Plyboo—flat-grained, natural-bamboo flooring for the kitchen, dining, and living areas. There is a colorful mix of several surface and cabinetry materials in the kitchen. To one side of the stove, the owner and architect designed a cast-concrete, rounded peninsula with a bullnosed edge inlaid with sea glass in a spiral pattern. A maple butcher-block counter was designed for the work surface on the other side of the stove. The countertop on the opposite side of the kitchen is made of plastic laminate. All of these contemporary materials are compatible with the bamboo-plank flooring where a quarter-round bamboo-strip base molding joins the floor and wall.

When southern California architect Kirk Gradin remodeled his home, he chose a sustainable palette of natural materials for millwork and finishes. The custom kitchen cabinetry is milled from multi-ply bamboo. Bamboo tambour softens and warms the look of the refrigerator doors. Slate tiles cover the floor and are used for the concrete counter's backsplash. The island's cabinetry is milled from bamboo with a round maple butcher-block work surface.

Architect Gradin's eat-at counter separates the kitchen and dining spaces. The front panel that faces the dining room is constructed of multi-ply bamboo. Tall bar stools made of wood with plaited-bamboo seat and back panels are available from Pier 1 Imports and match the dining chairs.

Versatile bamboo utensils are useful in eco-conscious kitchens, from chopsticks and paddles to a bamboo steamer for the stovetop. A bamboo scoop can be used for the tea, which could be steeped in a bamboo tea strainer and served in a ceramic *raku* teapot with a curved bamboo handle. For a special occasion, Japanese tea can be served in a ceremony that includes frothing the tea with a bamboo whisk.

In the home of a southern California architect, bamboo is one of the surface materials, but not the only one. Slate tiles for the floor and for the concrete countertop's backsplash complement the custom kitchen cabinetry milled from Plyboo. Bamboo tambour (narrow strips glued to a fabric backing) softens the look and warms the feel of the refrigerator doors.

The bamboo theme extends into the dining area, beginning with the front panel of the eat-at counter. The tall bar stools are wood, with bamboo seats and back panels. In the adjacent dining area, the chairs and table are designed in the same wood-and-bamboo style.

An Asian-influenced armoire with bamboo panels continues the melody, sitting with a stately presence in the corner at an angle to the room. Underfoot, the bamboo flooring is a grounding element in the dining space as it flows into the informal living room.

The architect-owner designed the two prominent bamboo furniture pieces in the living area. The half-round tambour-surfaced entertainment center is positioned to extend out from the slate-tiled fireplace at the same angle, or it can be rotated so the entertainment equipment is out of view. This is an attractive and clever design solution to the ever-present audio- and video-electronics dilemma. The interior of the center is constructed with bamboo shelving and bamboo pole supports.

To lift the weighty appearance of the concrete-topped coffee table with a tambour-skinned base, the architect designed a subtle reveal where the table meets the bamboo floor.

Bamboo in several forms—full culm, half culm, weaving, and planking—has a definite presence and adds a warm ambiance to another California ranch home. A pair of decorative bamboo columns, extending

Architect Kirk Gradin designed this half-round, tambour-skinned entertainment center for his renovated home. Here it is positioned to extend at an angle from the slate-tiled fireplace. The wheeled unit can also be rotated so that the electronic equipment is out of view while the rounded tambour surface faces outward. This is an attractive and practical solution for the ubiquitous audio and video electronics. Set back from the shelf edges, full-culm bamboo pieces provide shelf support.

A cast-concrete-topped living room coffee table was also designed by architect Kirk Gradin. Bamboo tambour wraps around the circular table base and is detailed with a reveal at the bottom where the furniture piece meets the golden-hued prefinished bamboo floor planks.

The altar table made by high-end furniture manufacturer McGuire welcomes you in this entry niche of a southern California luxury beachfront condominium designed by Ann James. The table legs are crafted from bundled small-diameter, dark colored bamboo wrapped with natural bamboo split straps. A black iron framework that fastens to the tops of the bamboo legs supports the hardwood tabletop. The modern circular mirror frame is carved from hardwood in a subtle bamboo motif. The woven-bamboo case beneath the table adds to the attractive vignette.

Facing: Interior decorator Ann James stylishly appointed the multipurpose den/study/guest room with contemporary furniture and accessories. A soft fabric-cushioned sofa is recessed into a ledged niche. Ann designed the continuous and functional ledge where lamps, artwork, artifacts, books and whatever can rest. Moving forward into the room, the timber-bamboo-framed coffee table's top is bamboo slats, made by crushing, splitting, and opening the culm. A woven-grass side armchair with fabric seat cushion sits comfortably in this environmentally friendly setting.

The kitchen entry is framed by timber-bamboo supports between the cabinet counters and shelving above. Bamboo flooring extends into the kitchen from the dining and living areas.

from the countertop to the upper shelving, flank the entry to the kitchen. Another pair of half-culm vertical poles, cut to fit between the stone hearth and the underside of the wooden mantel, frame the fireplace. A natural, prefinished bamboo floor covers the walking surface in the kitchen, dining, and living rooms, and extends down the halls.

At a beachfront condominium, the entry niche is furnished with an altar table that is supported by a bamboo base. Dark, thin bamboo is bundled together with bamboo straps, and steel connectors join the bamboo to the hardwood top. A similar design is repeated in a pair of side tables in the living room, where the bamboo base is shorter and the tabletop is travertine. In the study, a woven fabric gives the walls and the front of the Murphy bed texture, pattern, and dimension. Complementing the décor, the dark brown coffee-table legs and frame are crafted from full culms. Split bamboo pieces make up the table's surface.

Bamboo in the Bathroom and Bedroom

With a few beautiful bamboo gestures, an otherwise cold and hard-surfaced bathroom can be transformed into a soothing comfort zone. The South Seas ambiance in a powder room is created with a real ocean view. (You could re-create the scene with a faux painting or a photograph.) Here, a huge shell becomes the sink, two shell-collection displays are inset into the bamboo counter, and the walls are woven bamboo.

Another combination you might consider is a bamboo window shade for visual interest and wall texture, along with a woven bamboo hamper and a bamboo basket to soften finishes of linoleum flooring, milk-painted walls, and natural-stained wood cabinetry.

Any edges of bamboo flooring that are close to a tiled shower, water closet, or sink cabinet need to be carefully sealed with a water-resistant clear silicone.

Frequently applying coats of liquid resin is a good idea to keep the water continuously beading up on the floor.

A Pacific Island powder room designed by Corinna Gordon features a shell sink imported from the Philippines. The bracketed downlight over the sink is a Gordon original, crafted from giant-timber bamboo. The woven wall covering is made from split bamboo.

Several natural materials create an earthy ambiance in a private island residence's master bathroom. Woven bamboo covers the ceiling, while bamboo matting texturizes the walls and absorbs moisture from one's feet after a tub soak.

The cantilevered ceramic sink in the master bathroom with its bamboo pole supports—one at each corner—is unique. Where the bamboo culm meets the linoleum flooring, a silicone bead is an essential ingredient, giving the bamboo poles two pairs of boots where the water contact potential is considerable. The three graduated-sized culm vases show off the versatility of this great grass.

Zen-bamboo selective simplicity continues from the bath into the sleeping room.

The sleeping and dreaming zone in a canyon home is nicely arranged with lightweight fabric curtains hanging from a bamboo bed frame. The bed is level with the window that looks out to the canyon. A potted bamboo on the deck creates a compatible transition from indoors to out. This is a meditative spot for the homeowner, where she listens to bamboo music and sometimes writes bamboo poems.

Grab a colorful drink with a little bamboo-umbrella garnish, close your eyes, and imagine a tropical paradise. Perhaps you would conjure up a giant-timber bamboo bed sitting on a bamboo platform. Looking out from the four-poster bed, you visualize a closet that is made of split and woven bamboo. The top of the wardrobe is built at an angle to keep unwanted critters from making this territory their homestead. The sides of the storage unit are also slanted, carrying through the sloped design. At sunset, a light fixture crafted from timber bamboo glows warmly.

A stuffed panda bear rests comfortably in a bamboo haven: a bamboo bed frame with scrim curtains and a plaited bamboo screen defining the bed zone. Through the window one can view potted bamboo plants on the outside deck.

In another scenario (see p. 99), a high-rising, four-poster bamboo bed, complete with a scrim of mosquito netting, nestles on an angle to the room. Next to the bed, a bamboo dresser, constructed of woven bamboo panels and built with a clothes hamper tilt-out, anchors that part of the multifunctional space. Bamboo matchstick shades add some privacy to this comfortable, warm, and mellow "change of pace" place. This Caribbean "Island Ambiance" is available in the Caribbean for vacation stays (see Sourcebook.)

Facing: Bamboo basically dominates from this viewpoint: a bamboo-crafted lantern sits on a full- and split-culm tray; potted living bamboo sits on the outside deck. A whole collection of things bamboo are BambooMessengerWoman's interpretation of a Pacific Rim style for a bamboozled home interior.

This canopy bed was designed and built by Richard Dansey (Danscor) in the Philippines and imported to Australia by **BambooFurniture.com.au**. At the head and foot, the top rails of the bamboo sunburst pattern are constructed with a subtle camber. The four posts and canopy are made from timber bamboo with a soft fabric billowing at the top and head of the bed. The nightstands and their light fixture lamp bases are crafted in the same bamboo style.

Bamboo Outside

As a building material, bamboo can be incorporated into the outdoors of one's home environment in a variety of ways. Cut poles can vertically divide space, adding visual interest and giving privacy. A bamboo bridge can link two areas over a body of water or a dry gully. Bamboo can be used to create a "room with a view" at ground level or up a tree.

The widely spaced vertical and horizontal grid of this fence and gate is visually an open barrier. The architectonic design is both an attractive and functional space divider for the garden.

Neighboring Fences

Bamboo fencing is traditional as well as innovative. For centuries it has been used in Asia both decoratively and functionally. Living fences of bamboo define property boundaries, provide privacy, and nicely complement harvested bamboo fences.

The degree of privacy desired influences the design style of a harvested fence. A see-through fence can be a latticework with different amounts of openness in the weave. Traditional fences are often constructed of split bamboo that is woven in a horizontal pattern. These are available from fence

A variety known as *Bambusa multiplex*—Hedge Bamboo—is regularly shaped and trimmed. With minimal maintenance, the privacy screen is an effective and attractive hedgerow along a public way.

An original bamboo fence design by bamboo artist Beverly Messenger consists of orthogonal vertical and horizontal cut culms layered over panels of closely spaced reeds fitted into a wooden frame. The attractive effect creates a dense screen, blocking unsightly "back of the house" elements in the yardscape.

importers and manufacturers throughout the U.S. (see Sourcebook). Other bamboo fences are custom designed for specific locations.

Beyond a fence, bamboo can look good and work well in the garden. Cut stems create a bamboo framework of supports for tomato plants, snap peas, pole beans, or other edibles. Split bamboo, bent and formed into small arches and then placed directly into the soil, give buoyancy to crawling vines such as melons, cucumbers, or strawberries. Similar small arching bamboo stems are useful for defining an edge along a garden pathway.

Building Bamboo Bridges

Bamboo is strong, resilient, curvaceous, lightweight, and flexible, making it an excellent material for a railing or a bridge. Substantial and complex engineering enables a bridge to successfully span from one side of the riverbank to the other.

A railing is a short version of a fence that's built to withstand building-code requirements for a certain load or force per square inch. As with fence designs, railings can be made of a dense weave, or simple vertical and horizontal whole culms, or split bamboo rails. They can be placed along an uneven garden walkway or over a footbridge.

California bamboo artist Stephen Glassman, together with Colombian bamboo architect Oscar Hidalgo, directed Balinese builders to create this masterpiece of a footbridge over a sacred river gorge at Linda Garland's Panchoran estate. The Sylvia Campuan bamboo bridge, made of gracefully arching split culms as well as strong and straight full-diameter cut stalks, was built as a temporary structure for the 1995 Bamboo Festival.

Inspired by the traditional arched bamboo bridges of the Paez Indians, Colombian engineer Jörg Stamm constructed this covered bridge in Pereira, Colombia. *Guadua angustifolia*, the bamboo native to the Andean highlands between Ecuador and Venezuela, is used to create prefabricated trusses that were site-assembled to span more than 170 feet (52 meters). A small truck can navigate across the 9-foot (2.8-meter) width. The bridge's roof helps protect against harsh weather conditions of severe storms, heavy winds, and extreme temperatures. Stamm's eco-engineering with a low energy technology resulting in a high-tech solution displays the beauty of bamboo in a remarkable structural achievement. The complex arched truss and the bridge's static performance demonstrate the notion that form follows function.

Outdoor Bamboo Structures

Enter the garden through a bamboo gate. The bamboo wind chime hanging on the gate vocalizes as the gate swings, announcing arrivals and departures. A more elaborate and expressive formal portico or pergola can provide protection over the entry door—a dry place to open your umbrella.

The garden can be enhanced by a bamboo archway that supports vining plants. A trellis concept combines several pergola segments to form a support structure for those plants and to be a source of shade in the garden as well. To create a living bamboo trellis from young shoots, the growth can be trained onto a sculptural form. You can leave the understructure (a metal, wooden, or cut-bamboo framework) in place as the bamboo continues to grow, or you can remove it once the bamboo is forming the intended design.

During a weekend workshop at the Wright Way Organic Resource Center in Malibu, California, a group of students learned how to cut, craft, and fasten bamboo together. Bay Area architect Darrel DeBoer instructed the participants how to use the proper tools to work effectively and efficiently with bamboo. After two days of hands-on design and construction, the group positioned the two bamboo struts on their foundation and tied them together with bamboo poles to create the roof

Dave Flanagan, the Bamboo Fencer, located in Jamaica Plain, Massachusetts, has created a peaceful garden setting of living and harvested bamboos. The cut-culm fences are designed in a Japanese style called *Kenninji-gaki,* named after the Kenninji temple in Kyoto where it is said to have first been constructed. The closely spaced vertical bamboo pieces tied together with horizontal lengths provide considerable beauty and privacy.

A single fence panel of bamboo branches and twigs in the Japanese style called *Takeho-gaki* is a focal point at the end of the garden's stone pathway. Along the walk, a *shishi odoshi,* or "deer scarer" fountain adds a kinetic motion and rhythmic sound as the empty bamboo tube rotates to its original position, landing on the stone with a "clack." A bamboo arbor between the fountain and the fence panel adds vertical dimension as well as support for climbing vines. This sacred garden space's environment is enhanced with the planting of several bamboo species. The whole scheme represents bamboo in balance—living and harvested.

A garden shade structure was built by participants during a weekend bamboo workshop at the Wright Way Organic Resource Center in Malibu, California. Architect Darrel DeBoer instructed the group in bamboo cutting and fastening. Together they assembled the framework and secured it to the concrete footings. The structural skeleton was to be sheathed later with a roofing material, providing shelter from the sun and rain.

Hawaiian compact shelters come in a kit of parts requiring assembly—as does most IKEA furniture. These structures are being erected on the cluster of Pacific islands as well as on the mainland. Small constructions, no larger than a ten-by twelve-foot floor area (120 square feet), are fun and challenging backyard projects—a great place for a creative spirit to build a garden trellis, shade structure, small greenhouse, tree house, or doghouse.

Be advised that a local building permit may be required for such a project.

rafters of the structure. The framework was completed during the weekend. Others were recruited to add roofing material that would minimize wind uplift and provide dense solar shading under the structure.

A gazebo constructed of bamboo can provide a focal point in the garden. Kits are available that include prefab bamboo-panel structures, made by Bamboo Hardwoods in Maui and from Hammacher Schlemmer catalog, among others. You can construct your own or commission a skilled bamboo designer and a bamboo constructor to build one.

"Buddy's Bamboo Bungalow" is a terrific example of bamboo "barkitecture." Frank Chang, a policeman in Washington State, made the main doghouse from wood and the porch from bamboo, for Buddy—his German Shepherd, a police dog of course. In Frank's own words:

I never imagined that a doghouse could possibly wind up on a coffee table . . . Even though I have attained several milestones, I am most proud of that doghouse . . . my most enlightening achievement. It is two rooms—five by six by three-and-a-half feet. It sports a double roof with the polycarbonate top mounted to a removable frame. The 'interior' roof/ceiling is split and hinged for easy cleaning. The decking is split bamboo and is fastened on the ends with bamboo skewer "nails." The bridge also has split bamboo decking and actually crosses over a pond. It took five months to build.

The doghouse was originally built on a concrete patio, then placed on three-inch-diameter by twelve-foot-long bamboo poles and "rolled" (just like the Egyptians did) about forty feet across the lawn to its current location.

Policeman Frank Chang built "Buddy's Bamboo Bungalow" for his German Shepherd. It's a "pretty awesome doghouse . . . for a pretty good dog," says Chang. Bamboo poles are fashioned into gateways, railings, and porch-roof supports. Split bamboos are used for the decking and bamboo skewers are the "nails."

Lofty Bamboo Constructions

Expressed with extreme imagination, two bamboo tree houses have risen to wild heights.

Jo Scheer's tree house, "Hooch," was inspired by and named after the simple shelters built by Vietnamese peasant farmers. While the tree house is considerably different from the primitive shelters, they are similar in their simplicity and economy of space. Scheer wanted to build a structure that was separate from but accessible to his home. He started with an existing concrete septic tank, measuring five by seven feet, as the foundation base. He figured that he could angle the bamboo out from the base to create a platform measuring twice the area—ten by fourteen feet. "It became a master bedroom with a killer view," says Scheer. "The Hooch has survived several hurricanes. . . . The flexible nature of bamboo distributes any stress throughout the structure and thus minimizes failure. . . . The similarities of the design strategy of the Hooch and nature were hard to dismiss, and were thus embraced."

This type of tree house could be built in almost any location, could fit almost any tree, and could be a simple, low-impact, and easily erected prefab or on-site construction.

The Ba House was designed by Fernau & Hartman Architects, Inc., in San Francisco for an Asian garden. In "Improvisations on an Asian Theme," they write:

> Ba *roughly translates from the Japanese as "place." The two materials, Asian bamboo and milled Southeast Asia hardwood, have a "raw" and "cooked" contrast that accentuates the qualities of both. The main structural elements are constructed from unfinished bamboo—an incredibly strong*

This "master bedroom with a killer view" was designed and built by Jo Scheer as part of a Caribbean tree house he calls the "Hooch," named after a Vietnamese peasant shelter. The primary structure is bamboo poles and the railing's side panels are made of woven splits of bamboo.

Bottom: Water spilling from a bamboo spout fills the soak tub that anchors the master bedroom suite located high above the ground in Scheer's bamboo tree house. Imagine relaxing here in a tropical twilight setting at day's end, or at sunrise, enveloped in a soothing transition from sleep.

material—lighter than birds' bones . . . connected by means of cord lashings . . . canvas hammocks are slung over the bamboo joists and the corrugated concrete roof . . . caps the structure. . . . The raised vegetal rod structure is nestled into the foliage and sits lightly on the ground.

Outdoor Sculptures

Bamboo art in public spaces attracts lots of people. Several European locations were the sites for temporary charismatic bamboo constructions for public viewing—a large bamboo sculpture in Berlin was doubly impressive with its image seen in a reflecting pool. At Carwinion in the United Kingdom, Antoon Versteegde from the Netherlands created a huge, circular Ferris wheel–type of bamboo sculpture by joining the pieces together with rubber bands.

San Francisco architects Fernau & Hartman designed this Asian-inspired tree house for the Strybing Arboretum in Golden Gate Park. Bamboos are the main structural elements. Milled tuan, a hardwood from New Guinea, was used to construct the moveable walls, a fold-down table, and the floorboards. The "Ba House," as it is called, was sensitively designed for the site and climate: roof overhangs protect the structure from sun and rain; air freely flows through the slatted wall panels, which can be hoisted for the views or lowered for privacy.

Joining pieces of bamboo together with rubber bands, Dutch sculptor Antoon Versteegde constructed this Ferris wheel–type sculpture at Carwinion in the United Kingdom.

Japanese architect Akio Hizume designs and constructs *Starcage* bamboo sculptures. His avant-garde blend of science and art demonstrates quasi-periodic, geometric creations based on the Golden Mean. This *Starcage* is located at the Bamboo Giant nursery in Aptos, California, where *Ilostachus vivax* and Giant Black Bamboo (*Phyllostachys nigra "Daikokuchiku"*) provide the living-bamboo backdrop.

Artist-Sculptor Stephen Glassman created *Koi Sticks (fish out of water)* using three types of split and shaved bamboos: beechey bamboo (*Bambusa beecheyana*), madake (*Phyllostachys bambusiodes*), and golden bamboo (*Phyllostachys aurea*). In this sculpture (30" x 30" x 8') approximately fifteen pounds of bamboo support nearly 150 pounds of slumped glass. The structural bones of bamboo articulate a transparent volume of the image of koi—an icon of Zen meditation. Glass has the molecular structure of liquid and is termed a "disorganized solid." One ponders where does the fish end and the water begin.

Southern Californian public artist-sculptor Stephen Glassman fully embraces bamboo in his art and philosophy. In "Public Intent: Bamboo Siteworks," a 2001 Chrysler Design Awards catalog, he states:

> *Bamboo . . . allows me to work on an architectural scale with the gesture and spontaneity of drawing, and led me to the creation of "temporary monumental site work." . . . Bamboo's strength and beauty are only a manifestation of its underground decentralized and horizontal hierarchical structure . . . deriving its strength from its unity and connectedness. . . . Bamboo is a model for social and technological structure that has existed for centuries in ancient bamboo cultures, but it is only just beginning to enter the Western world.*

Growing Your Own Bamboo

Living with living bamboo allows more than a thousand choices of species. Some variety of bamboo can be grown in almost all geographical areas, whether in the landscape or in a container. Bamboos' statures and sizes range from low-growing ground covers to sky-reaching stalks of various thicknesses.

Bamboo plantings serve several functions. A grove of bamboo is an oasis from intense sun; where the temperature can be ten degrees cooler than outside the forest. Planted in the landscape, it can be used as a screen or a fence—to soften a sharp angle or corner of a property, to bring vitality and variety into the yardscape, and to provide a visual transition from indoors to outdoors when planted in a pot and set out on a patio or terrace.

As you make plans for incorporating living bamboo into your environment, think about how you want the bamboo to be in the landscape—as a screen or fence? as a trimmed hedge? as a ground cover? Do you have room for a small bamboo plantation? Is a collection of potted plants preferable to plants in the ground?

In most outdoor spaces adjacent to a residence, a desirable bamboo planting in the ground would be either a clumping bamboo species or a contained runner variety. Glazed ceramic, metal, or stone containers are suitable, practical, and attractive vessels for potted bamboo plants. They come in a variety of sizes, as do the bamboos.

A study of your location for year-round climatic conditions, soils,

A planting of *Chusquea culeou* species is a good choice where density is desired in a landscape. Multiple branches with tight clustering of leaves are found at each node of the bamboo. As the culm sheaths begin to peel away from the stalk, a rich green color is revealed.

and drainage will help you discover which species is a good choice for you to plant. An excellent resource for learning about bamboo species and their growing requirements is the "Sourcelist," published annually by the American Bamboo Society and available in printed and down-loadable form from *www.americanbamboo.org*. (Other references and sources of information for growing bamboo are noted in the Sourcebook with an *.) Think globally but act locally.

You'll want to consider the characteristics of the bamboo: Is it a clumper or a runner? What is the culm size—diameter and height; the culm and leaf color; the form, shape, texture; and the bamboo's branching patterns?

A low ground cover planting of *Pleioblastus fortunei*, with white and green variegated leaves, creates a soft textural layer in the foreground, contrasting with Narihira bamboo (*Semiarundinaria fastuosa*) a dark-green-leafed, tall and stately bamboo in the background.

Propagation and Planting

Before setting the plant in the ground, it is important to consider where it is being planted—elevation, exposure to sun and wind, and slope—and what soil type and drainage conditions exist in that setting. Bamboos like to be protected from wind, and some will thrive in partial rather than full sun. Bamboos do not like poorly drained soils.

Most plant starts have their origins in seeds that grow into seedlings. For bamboos—most of which flower irregularly and infrequently and have limited seed production—the common practice is to propagate from cut subterranean rhizome sections or cut culms that include branches. For both temperate and tropical species, this vegetative propagation method is the most effective way to establish bamboos in a garden or in a grove. A bamboo cloned in this way will send out spring shoots after a year or so in the ground or container.

It is best to plant temperate (running) bamboos between October and December (in the Northern Hemisphere). Tropical (clumping) bamboos should be planted at the beginning of the rainy season—spring to early summer. In either case, bamboos favor warm, moist soils. When digging the hole for your planting, it is beneficial to break up the soil around the edges and to amend the soil with organic mulch and fertilizer. Be sure the bottom of the hole allows water to pass through and disperse into the surrounding ground. Add stones, rocks, gravel, or sand to the bottom to improve the drainage.

If you are transplanting a bamboo from a container, dig the hole three to six inches deeper than the original pot. Place the plant in the hole and fill with soil. A high-nitrogen bonemeal-type fertilizer will encourage the new bamboo's growth. Because the underground stem system is fairly shallow, place the fertilizer in the top six to eight inches of soil. In well-drained soil, create a slight depression or saucer at the surface to help with water retention, ensuring that the water reaches the newly planted bamboo's rhizome and roots. In wet soils, mound the dirt around the base of the plant to allow excess water to run off and away from the roots. This will help prevent too much water sitting in one place.

During the first few years in its new location, regular water soakings will aid the bamboo in getting established. After planting, add to the surface an organic mulch of

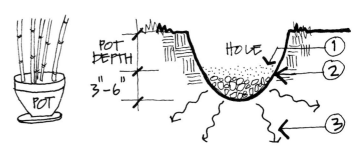

① STONES, ROCKS, GRAVEL, SAND

② BREAK UP SOIL AROUND THE EDGES

③ WATER DISPERSING EASILY INTO THE SOIL

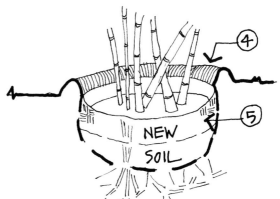

④ IN WELL-DRAINED SOIL, CREATE A SLIGHT SAUCER DEPRESSION TO HOLD WATER SO IT REACHES OUT TO THE UNDERGROUND RHIZOMATIC NETWORK

⑤ ADD A HIGH-NITROGEN BONE-MEAL TYPE FERTILIZER & ORGANIC MULCH

⑥ IN WET SOILS, MOUND THE DIRT AROUND THE BASE OF THE PLANT TO ALLOW EXTRA WATER TO RUN-OFF & AWAY FROM THE ROOTS

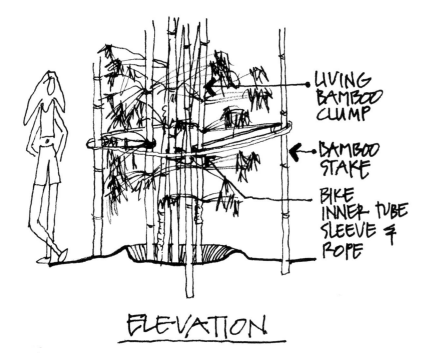

ELEVATION

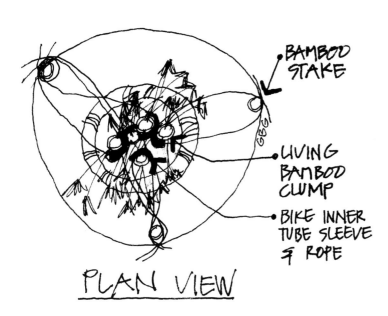

PLAN VIEW

leaves and compost to help keep the soil warm and moist.

If you are planting a relatively tall specimen in an open site with heavy winds, the bamboo welcomes structural support until it is sturdy enough to stand on its own. To provide support, place three cut bamboo stakes in an equally spaced triangular arrangement around the bamboo. Gently tie a natural rope fiber around both the growing bamboo and the stakes. To add more protection to the outermost culm surface, pass the rope through a suitable length of bicycle inner tube and then position the rubber sleeve around the culm.

Bamboo growers have observed the following: during the first year, the newly planted bamboo "sleeps"; the second year it "creeps," and by the third year, it "leaps."*

The emerging shoot, which comes fully programmed with all its DNA intact and spends its first eight to ten weeks above ground heading upward, will have a diameter that is bigger than all the other culms in the cluster or running from the mother. This new culm will also be taller than all the existing culms.

*Carol Miles, Chuhe Chen, Tamera Flores, "On-Farm Bamboo Production in the Pacific Northwest," *Bamboo: The Magazine of the American Bamboo Society*, August 2001, p. 12.

After the culm has finished its vertical growth spurt, the branches extend and leaf out. Prior to the branches coming out at the nodes, they are carefully tucked away and protected by the culm sheath—a heavy leaf-like "cardigan" that shields the new stalk from too much initial exposure to the world. The culm sheath hugs the branch close to the stalk and provides nutrients during the growing process.

Given good growing conditions—good weather and rain, nutritious soil, and tender loving care—most bamboos will shoot for five to ten years. Such a mature grove will continue to produce new shoots annually, and they will be similar in diameter and height to the already developed culms. But not all of the new shoots will have the same character: if a culm doesn't receive adequate food, it might grow smaller or shorter than its neighbors.

As the bamboo grows and matures, the culms that are the largest around and tallest in height are also the youngest in age. So, being an older bamboo doesn't mean being a bigger bamboo, as in the case of a tree. Because it is different from a tree's physiology with which we are familiar, bamboo physiology can be initially confusing.

BAMBOO MATURING

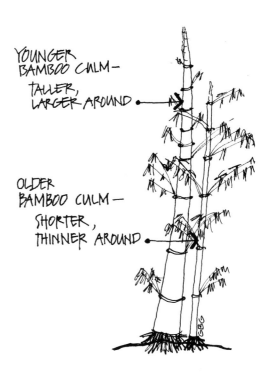

YOUNGER BAMBOO CULM— TALLER, LARGER AROUND

OLDER BAMBOO CULM— SHORTER, THINNER AROUND

Left: The culm sheaths of this Blue Bamboo (*Himalayacalamus hookerianus*) clump, growing at the Bamboo Sourcery in northern California, protect the bamboo's outside surface during its initial growth. As the stalk becomes sturdier, these coverings release and fall to the ground, providing nutritious mulch.

Right: A *Phyllostachys* bamboo shoot, recently emerged from the ground and extended skyward with its thickness fixed, will reach its full potential in just six to eight weeks of growing time.

A living plant that is popularly sold under the name "lucky bamboo" and grows in water isn't really bamboo at all, but belongs to the *Dracaena* family of plants, specifically *Dracaena*

sanderana. Lucky bamboo has just a few leaves at its top, and its jointed stems look similar to bamboo. The more valuable lucky bamboos have stems with multiple curls—a growth pattern forced by limiting its exposure to light. It is not a hardy plant and not suitable for the outdoors. To encourage positive feng shui, the Chinese will give a lucky bamboo plant at a housewarming, at the opening of a new business, or on the Chinese New Year.

Troubleshooting

Your bamboo will communicate its stresses or health conditions with signs similar to those of other plants. The following common symptoms indicate that the plant needs a change:

If	Then
Curled leaves, limited shoot production, diminished culm growth in summer	The bamboo needs more water, and a good soaker hose works very well.
Stunted growth	The bamboo needs more light or warmth.
Underdeveloped rhizome stems and weak rhizome foundation	The bamboo needs more warmth.
Withering	The bamboo is getting too much sun.
Failure to thrive	The bamboo needs better soil and drainage.

Pruning and Thinning Bamboo

To keep the growth looking vital and healthy, once a year you should cut out older culms that are discolored, damaged, or dead. Dead culms are khaki in color and lack any new green growth. By thinning out the culms, clumping bamboos receive more sunlight and air circulation, both of which are critical to the plant's vigorous growth. When culms are given decent breathing room, they thrive independently. Thinning bamboo clumps also protects adjacent canes from surface scraping—damage that can occur during severe weather conditions.

Because nutrients are at their lowest after spring shooting and the brittle culms snap during the growing season, the best times of the year to thin the mature culms are late summer, fall, and winter—from August until March in the Northern Hemisphere. But don't be too aggressive; remove only up to one third of the mature culms, as the remaining growth relies on neighboring stalks for physical support and shielding from prevailing winds.

You can take an ornamental approach to pruning by trimming the lower branches to expose a colorfully colored culm or one with an interesting shape and form. A good time to do this type of trimming is at the beginning stage of branch formation, when the branch is pliable and easily removed. If the bamboo is being groomed as a hedge or screen, prune the growth in the springtime to keep it well shaped and tidy. Bamboos look their best when errant branches, top-heavy growth, and weak or damaged culms are removed.

THICK CLUMP

PRUNE & THIN UP TO ⅓ OF DISCOLORED (KHAKI) CULMS OR MATURE CULMS

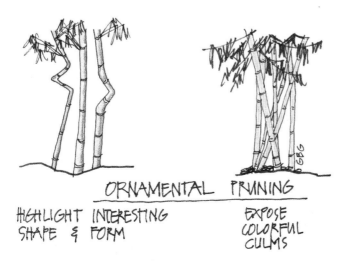

ORNAMENTAL PRUNING

HIGHLIGHT INTERESTING SHAPE & FORM

EXPOSE COLORFUL CULMS

Dividing the growth at the base is another technique to maintain the plant's pleasing proportions. This action will both improve the appearance and give the new plant division an opportunity to thrive in a new location. With potted bamboos, separate the rhizome system in half and repot each portion in a suitable container. Transplanting a new division can be done at any time of the year, except when new shoots are emerging. When you divide the plant, use a wrap of burlap or plastic sheeting to keep a root ball of soil around the rhizome and roots. During this process, keep the root ball wet.

Bamboo does attract an unwanted pest—the bamboo mite *(Schizotetranychus celarius)*. If the bamboo mite finds its way into your garden, it is a difficult pest to eradicate. When introducing a new bamboo, inspect the leaves carefully for yellow blotches or scarring. If rectangular spots resembling a Morse code pattern are found on the margin and midribs of the leaf, bamboo mite is present. According to Robin Rosetta, an entomologist at Oregon State University, mite management consists of inspection, quarantine, and eradication. She recommends treating the mite with biological predators or pesticide sprays, reminding us that if we kill a natural enemy, we inherit its work. You can also try to eliminate mites by "clear-cutting," whereby you remove all the foliage from the infested plant. The best time to clear-cut is in late winter or early spring.

Controlling Growth

Running bamboos—most of the temperate species—have the reputation of being invasive, pesty plants that grow out of control, especially when they travel beyond your boundaries and unwontedly into a neighbor's yard.

By preparing the ground with a sturdy, heavy plastic sheeting made of high-density polyethylene as a barrier and placed about two to three feet below the soil surface, it is much easier to contain the long and zealous horizontal runs of the underground rhizome. Proper joining together of the plastic barrier segments is mandatory for successful control. Securely bolt the barrier together with a stainless-steel closure strip where the ends meet. A closure strip costs around fifteen dollars.

The tenacious plant will find any weakness and force its way out. To keep the stems from finding their way over the top, extend the lip of the barrier two to three inches above the ground surface. Plastic underground barriers are available at most bamboo nurseries and cost a couple of dollars per running foot. A poured-in-place concrete trench can also be an effective rhizome barrier. Either of these barriers requires careful monitoring and removal of any stray growth.

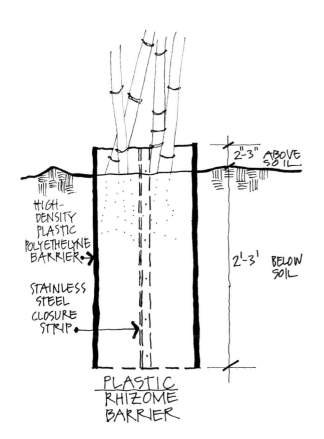

HIGH-
DENSITY
PLASTIC
POLYETHELYNE
BARRIER

STAINLESS
STEEL
CLOSURE
STRIP

2"-3" ABOVE
SOIL

2'-3' BELOW
SOIL

PLASTIC
RHIZOME
BARRIER

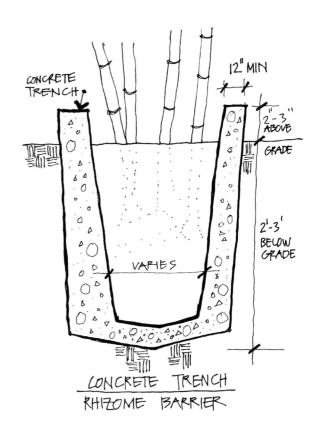

CONCRETE
TRENCH

12" MIN

2"-3"
ABOVE
GRADE

2'-3'
BELOW
GRADE

VARIES

CONCRETE TRENCH
RHIZOME BARRIER

Planting bamboo in a raised bed at least three feet high will help contain the horizontal underground stems that travel in a zone one-and-a-half to two feet below the soil surface. Restricting drip irrigation to the center of the plant offers another type of control, as the rhizomes like the humidity and prefer being close to the water source.

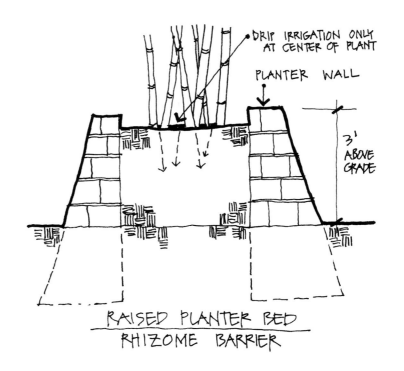

DRIP IRRIGATION ONLY
AT CENTER OF PLANT

PLANTER WALL

3'
ABOVE
GRADE

RAISED PLANTER BED
RHIZOME BARRIER

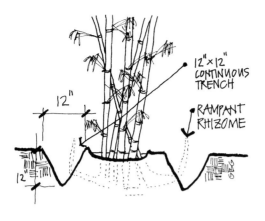

DUGDIRT TRENCH
RHIZOME BARRIER

In addition to providing a physical barrier, digging a foot-wide-by-foot-deep trench on either side of a running bamboo's path will help in monitoring the plant. The open swath is a trap of sorts: you can visually inspect the trench at the beginning of the shooting season to see if any rampant rhizome has escaped. In the springtime, step on newly emerging shoots or cut unwanted stems to keep growth in check. Since bamboos avoid salty seaweed, you could partially fill the trench with this material, which will likely help curb the plants' activity.

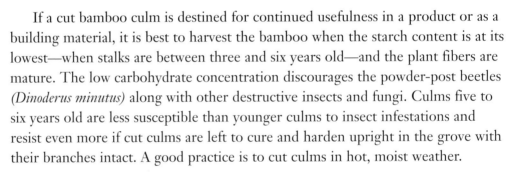

Harvesting Bamboo

If a cut bamboo culm is destined for continued usefulness in a product or as a building material, it is best to harvest the bamboo when the starch content is at its lowest—when stalks are between three and six years old—and the plant fibers are mature. The low carbohydrate concentration discourages the powder-post beetles (*Dinoderus minutus*) along with other destructive insects and fungi. Culms five to six years old are less susceptible than younger culms to insect infestations and resist even more if cut culms are left to cure and harden upright in the grove with their branches intact. A good practice is to cut culms in hot, moist weather.

After three to five years of initial growth, up to one-third of a grove can be cut annually with no harm to the bamboo forest, since the plant continues to produce new, hardy, strong, and flexible shoots. In comparison, it takes at least twenty-five years for a tree forest to mature and have its lumber felled for use.

Using the proper tools will make the task of cutting the culms easier. A reciprocating saw (a Sawzall) or a chain saw for really large, unwieldy growth is preferable to a handsaw typically used to cut wood. However, if you choose to cut by hand, a Japanese pull saw (also called a razorsaw) makes a clean, quick cut. Proper protection is a good idea—wear thick leather gloves and safety glasses.

After any severe cutting, a good dose of fertilizer applied to the bamboo will stimulate the remaining growth and encourage new shoot development.

Seasoning Bamboo

After the poles are cut, there are several ways to air-dry the bamboo: if left in the grove, the branches should remain intact with the culms arranged vertically so they support one another. Alternatively, trim all the branches and stack flat in an area that is protected and where the temperature is relatively cool. However, drying culms in the horizontal mode will take twice as long. If the culms are going to be split and crafted, it is best to use stalks that have been drying for six weeks—they will still retain some moisture, making bending and working with the material easier.

Kiln or oven drying of split culms speeds up the process by about two to three weeks and gives the harvester more control over the drying. This method is the preferred standard in the bamboo composite-manufacturing industry.

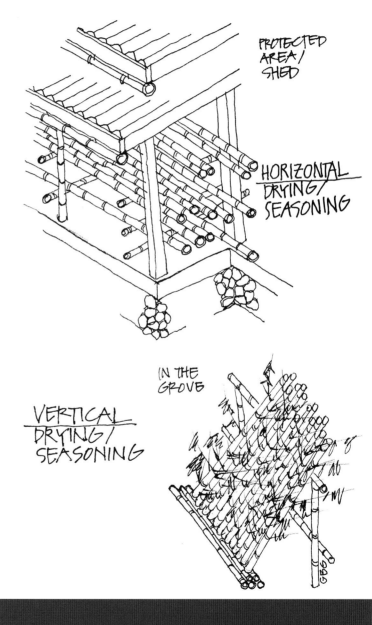

PROTECTED AREA / SHED

HORIZONTAL DRYING / SEASONING

IN THE GROVE

VERTICAL DRYING / SEASONING

AIR DRYING BAMBOO

Treating Bamboo

There are four methods for discouraging beetles that attack culms:

1. Soaking the culms in water is a cheap and effective way to reduce the carbohydrate content. The thicker the culm, the longer it needs soaking: around five to six weeks. The time factor is the biggest disadvantage to this method.

2. In the Boucherie method that has been refined and championed by the well-respected bamboo anatomy expert Dr. Walter Liese, professor emeritus at the University of Hamburg in Germany, a nontoxic solution of borax and water is forced through the bamboo culm's fibers, replacing the starchy carbohydrates.

3. A relatively new alternative treatment practiced in Indonesia is to vertically soak the canes. The internal nodes are punched out and the borate solution is poured into the hollow culms. Capillary action sucks up the solution and the anti-beetle results are reportedly good.

4. In Japan, the preferred methods of bamboo seasoning are sun and smoke. With the solar treatment, the cut culms are often bundled together in the open air and then leaned vertically against a rack to help each other dry in a straight position. The sun bakes the stalks and, in the process, the culms lose their starch and the beetles lose interest.

Cooking fires in the traditional Japanese kitchen are stoked in flueless ovens. Cut bamboo poles are placed in the raftered loft spaces above the kitchen, where they receive the fire's heat and smoke. Smoking is an effective culm-curing method and insect deterrent. This method darkens the culms, which also retain some of the smoky odor. These smoked culms are valued antiques. A modern smoking method of placing the cut culms vertically in an enclosed metal chamber is currently practiced in Japan and other countries.

Follow these time-honored ways to cut, cure, and season harvested bamboo to get the most out of bamboo buildings, furniture, and crafts. Bamboo fences, fountains, pergolas, benches, and bridges in the landscape will look good and last a long time if you treat the bamboo and practice a regular protective maintenance and care program.

VERTICAL SOAK

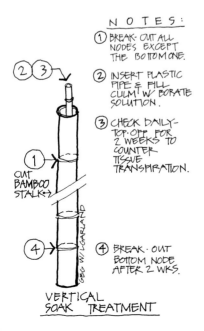

NOTES:

① BREAK-OUT ALL NODES EXCEPT THE BOTTOM ONE.

② INSERT PLASTIC PIPE & FILL CULM w/ BORATE SOLUTION.

③ CHECK DAILY- TOP-OFF FOR 2 WEEKS TO COUNTER TISSUE TRANSPIRATION.

CUT BAMBOO STALK→

④ BREAK-OUT BOTTOM NODE AFTER 2 WKS.

VERTICAL SOAK TREATMENT

Bamboo Giant nursery,
Aptos, California.

On Your Own

The examples from a few of the many talented bamboo fine artists featured in the Way of Bamboo chapter show a range of bamboo possibilities that they've done *on their own*. Hopefully, they are an inspiration for you to explore bamboo possibilities *on your own*. One way for you to get answers about bamboo is to have a hands-on experience: Attend a workshop led by seasoned professionals using seasoned bamboo, and then practice on your own.

As with most anything, it is important to have the right tools when you're working with bamboo. Hacksaws will do just that—and the bamboo will look awful and neither of you will be happy. A Japanese razorsaw, however, will do the job cleanly. Splitters are good tools to have—one that looks like an apple section cutter and another like a hand-held butcher-type knife. Two good places to get your tools are Bamboo-Smiths in Nevada City, California, and Hida Tools, a Japanese tool-supply company in Berkeley, California (see Sourcebook—Marketplace).

Several talented bamboo constructors generously share their knowledge and creative projects so you can make your own.

An arched bamboo gateway arbor located in New England is a climbing structure for vining plants. The construction consists of full and split culms, both straight and bent.

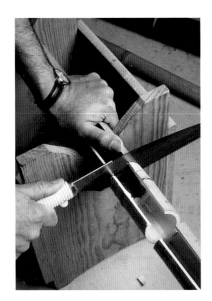

Cutting a culm at the Bamboo-Smiths.

Splitting a culm at a Bamboo-Smiths workshop.

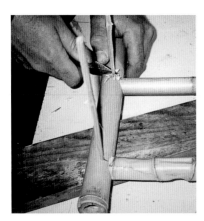

Fastening bamboos together at a Bamboo-Smiths workshop.

Bamboo-Smiths Doug and Martha Lingen, along with Reed Hamilton, have extensive experience building with bamboo. They share their knowledge in weekend workshops all across the nation. They teach basic bamboo skills: cutting a pole using a jig, splitting bamboo, and fastening bamboo. From personal experience, I highly recommend participating in one of their bamboo hands-on workshops.

Fascinating Bamboo Fastening

Joining either full culms or split bamboo pieces together is one of the biggest challenges of working and constructing with bamboo. How we build bamboo joints significantly impacts how we build with bamboo. In Asian cultures, bamboo has been joined to bamboo with bamboo: the larger-diameter full culms are joined by thin strips of split bamboo that secure one to the other. This method limits the structure's size to mostly a single level.

When two pieces of bamboo pass each other, they can be lashed together with woven fibers—hemp, jute, or linen. These materials will become less secure and deteriorate when exposed to the elements. The tying of joints, by itself, is not strong or durable enough. The joints weaken as the lashing material loosens, stretches, and becomes brittle. Within a couple of years, tightening of the rope—and possibly replacing it—will be necessary.

Bamboo builders in Pacific Rim countries lash with materials of other natural fibers. Coconut fibers called *tali* are used in Bali.

Ropes made of organic fibers or very thin splits of bamboo can be used to decorate a more substantial joint like one that uses steel bolts and concrete. In this case, the bamboo wrapping is a passive participant—all the work to fasten the joint together is done by the steel bolt-and-concrete combination. The steel passes through a bamboo node and is secured—not snugged down to a point of piercing the node's surface—to the inside of the bamboo culm via an access hole. Using the same access hole, a concrete mix then fills the hollow culm section that contains the steel bolt.

New construction methods of designing weight-bearing structural joinery are making bamboo a more viable material in the West, along with hardwoods from sustainably managed forests.

Some contemporary connections that are more weather-resistant are lashed with plastic and rubber in the form of bands, strips, and hosing. Bamboo construction pieces can be bolted together with stainless steel and electric conduit that's split in half.

Architect Simón Vélez prefers using a combination of steel bolts with concrete mortar to join full culms of bamboo together. He may also reinforce the joint by fastening steel straps at the most stressed locations, which helps reduce the natural tendency of the bamboo to crack and split. He uses a fish-mouth-shaped compression joint where the gravity forces are pushing downward. Shaped ends of roof rafters rest on a horizontal beam where the top of a wall meets a sloped roof/ceiling. The process of carving a fish-mouth takes practice, the right tools, good instruction, and plenty of skill. A fish-mouth joint *not* in compression needs mechanical fastening.

At Marcelo Villegas's iron foundry in Manizales, Colombia, metalworkers fashion a cast bronze fitting that follows the bamboo's curvature and makes it possible to create a tightly secured fastening and a handsome design solution.

Crafting bamboo furniture joints is also a challenge. In one furniture design, the material is carved so it can be in tension as it wraps around horizontal members at the connection. The carved culm then makes a ninety-degree angle and becomes the supporting leg, which is in compression.

A typical furniture joint made by Pacific Rim artisans uses thin bamboo splits to decoratively wrap the ends of the full culms thereby hiding the mechanical fasteners.

Suspended in the loft of an art gallery in Bogotá, Colombia, a "sleigh bed" built from lengths of *Guadua* rhizome rails and round macana-wood slats was designed and built by artisan Marcelo Villegas. The leather-bed platform is laced to the bamboo frame. Leather straps are connected to the bamboo by shaped bronze hardware connectors forged at Villegas's foundry and contoured to fit the bamboo.

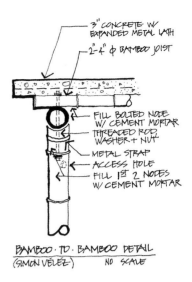

BAMBOO·TO·BAMBOO DETAIL
(SIMON VÉLEZ)   NO SCALE

A bamboo stool crafted in Vietnam has legs that begin as horizontal culms carved to create tensioned wrap-joints and then turn downward to become the vertical supports.

Bamboo architect, educator, and constructor Darrel DeBoer has created three projects for you to do on your own: a pen, a ladle, and a vase with a lid.

A ONE-MINUTE FOUNTAIN PEN

We're starting simple first, and although it may take more than a minute, you get the idea.

Species: Golden Bamboo (*Phyllostachys aurea*)

1 Common Golden Bamboo is a good choice because the diameter is small, the nodes near the bottom are compressed and look interesting.

2 Drill a small hole $1/2$ inch from the probable tip near a node. The indented groove, or sulcis, is a good spot to choose.

3 Split the bamboo down the center of the hole.

4 Cut partway through near the node, keeping the hole and slit.

5 Break out the waste.

6 Carve the tip.

7 Voilá.

LADLE

This project takes concentration and is made up of three separate parts: the bowl, the handle, and the "wedgie," or bamboo pin.

Species: Henon Bamboo (*Phyllostachys nigra 'Henon'*)

1 Use a traditional bamboo splitter, make the handle.

2 A butcher knife is an alternate splitter.

3 Use a marking knife to scrape off the sharp edges.

4 Drill an angled hole for the handle and hold it in place with a small bamboo pin.

5 To split small bamboo pins, brace the front of the butcher knife against the table. Sharpen the tip of the pin so the corners of the square pin will hold when inserted into the round hole.

6 Turn ladle over and insert pin where handle passes through culm.

7 Voilá.

A single exotic flower of the Georgia O'Keeffe variety would look stunning in this container, used as a central focus on a dining table. If you want to have the flower in water, insert a glass test tube or other similar glass container to hold the water.

Species: Black Bamboo (*Phyllostachys nigra*)

1 Trim the branches a bit long while in the bamboo grove.

2 After six weeks of seasoning, cut the culm to length— depending on how much support you want from the branches.

3 Cut off the lid. Choose a spot that's close to round.

5 Carefully deepen the score about half the wall thickness using a saw that will cut a minimal width.

6 Remove the waste with a chisel or gouge.

7 Score the inside using the exact same setting on the marking gauge.

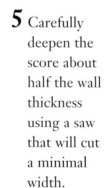

8 Remove the waste.

4 Score the outside for the base with either a Japanese- or English-style marking gauge.

9 Voilá.

A trained industrial designer, Gerard Minakawa, created this entry pergola for a natural-products resource center.

This is definitely a more complicated project. The pergola structure can be used at an entry to a home, shop, or garden retreat. You can construct a trellis by placing multiple sections of a pergola together in sequence.

Species: Black Bamboo (*Phyllostachys nigra*)

Golden Bamboo (*Phyllostachys aurea*) or other thin bamboo

Tools

- Razor saw
- Hammer
- $1/2$" chisel
- Power drill
- $3/8$" & $3/32$" Brad Point bits
- Utility or Exacto knife

Materials

- 3" diameter Black Bamboo
- 1" diameter Golden Bamboo poles
- 2 lbs Black coconut fiber rope
- 1 lb box 8d x $2^{1}/_{2}$" galvanized nails

1 Using a razorsaw, cut the 3"-diameter black bamboo to length. These poles will be used to construct the sides and top of the pergola.

2 Cut fishmouths into the ends of the bamboo to be used for the crossbeams.

3 Using a hammer and chisel, split the bamboo to make 12 dowels, each $1^{1}/_{2}$" longer than the diameter of the bamboo.

145

4 Using a Brad Point bit, drill a ³/8" hole within the cross-beam, 1" down from fish-mouth. Hammer the dowel into the hole. Using a utility knife, soften the dowel edges.

6 Finished lashings.

5 Using black coconut fiber rope, lash the pieces together. The dowel and rope together create tension of the crossbeam against the post.

7 Assemble the two sides and the top of the pergola.

8 Attach the top to the sides. Make 4 dowels the length of 2 bamboo diameters plus 1¹/2". Insert the dowels at 4 points. Reinforce the joints with square lashings.

9 Assembled pergola before diagonal braces and rafters are attached.

Notes

• Hand-select the bamboo poles.
• Since the Black Bamboo provides all the structural support for the pergola, the screening pattern can be your choice. In this case, the designer chose the golden bamboo poles to provide a contrasting color and a sense of pattern and rhythm to the outside surface.

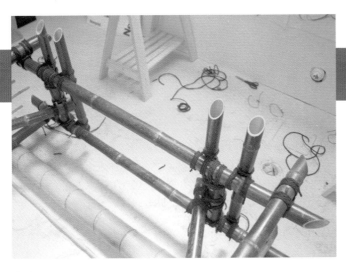

10 To complete the top, set the pergola on its side. Attach the four rafters—the short vertical pieces with the sawed-off ends—to the top with dowels and square lashings. On each side, attach a diagonal brace with dowels and square lashings. NOTE: The braces will be connected to a rafter and the upper crossbeam of the sides.

12 Detail of the screen pattern.

11 For the decorative screening, a series of 1" diameter golden bamboo poles are arranged to resemble organ pipes. Cut the poles to their rough length. Pre-drill the poles with a $^3/_{32}$" Brad Point bit. Attach the poles with $2^1/_2$" x 8d galvanized finish nails, 2 per pole. Use only 2 nails per pole because the screening is non-structural.

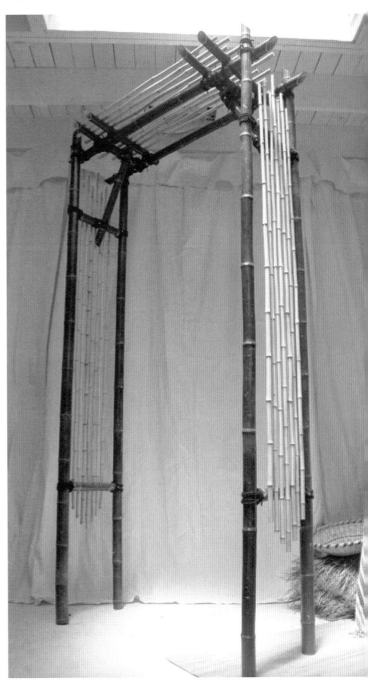

13 View of the finished pergola before securing in place.

Afterword: Bamboo and Beyond

Not a fading fad but a tenacious trend, bamboo is found at both ends of the retail marketplace—from tchotchke shops to high-end designer boutiques for furniture, art, and functional decorative objects. And in between, national import chains sell a wide range of bamboo products, from modern teak-and-bamboo furniture for home and office to crafted tea whisks and trays.

See for yourself. In the new international terminal at San Francisco International Airport, giant living Moso bamboo (*Phyllostachys heterocycla pubescens*) plantings are stretching upwards more than thirty feet. These elegant stalks will soon fill the empty space of a fifty-foot vertical void. Laminated multi-ply bamboo millwork surrounds the displays at a Japanese restaurant in the terminal's food court.

The Internet is a tremendous facilitator of discussion and information exchange about bamboo. Craftspersons from all over the globe are posting examples of their artworks on the Web through the Yahoo! egroup for Bamboo Crafts. Wolfgang Eberts, who owns a bamboo nursery in Germany—Bambus-Centrum Deutchland—has requested scanned images of "1,000 Bamboo Things" to be posted on his Website, *www.bambus.de*. So far, he's gathered more than three hundred. Two additional active Internet bamboo communications groups, the American Bamboo Society-sponsored Internet Bamboo Group and another Yahoo! egroup, Bamboo Plantations, encourage discussions and sharing of bamboo questions and answers. All of these form a rhizomatic network of cyber connections comprising bamboo enthusiasts who have a finger on the electronic bamboo pulse.

Now the challenge is to put all of this knowledge to the highest and best use, starting at the grassroots level. An achievable goal in both underdeveloped and industrialized nations is to have the populations participate and be able to earn a living wage by growing, cultivating, harvesting, seasoning, treating, curing, crafting, and constructing with bamboo.

Not Just for Pandas

If more than half of the world's population grows and utilizes bamboo, including building structures for suitable shelter, then why not the other half? We are all potential farmers as well as designers and builders—given the right training, skills, and tools.

Historically, people's learning and experience has always included making a basic human shelter. With the worldwide chronic need for more housing, why not teach how to build one's own home alongside the basic skills of reading, writing, and arithmetic?

Post-disaster dwellings have benefited from active participation by architects, designers, and constructors in the rebuilding process. The increasing numbers of homeless—not only in underdeveloped nations, but right here in our urban front yards—should prompt us to seek suitable shelter solutions. The day-labor lines certainly include workers without homes. We can help people with their housing needs by teaching them to grow bamboo; to harvest, treat and cure bamboo; to work with bamboo; to use bamboo; and to build with bamboo.

Can we be activists at the local level to provide resources for housing solutions? Can we encourage government powers-that-be to establish bamboo plantations, and in the process, give people an education and livelihood? The notion of hands working together to provide something for all is a deeply rooted one: in primitive cultures in Asia, Africa, and India; in Israeli kibbutzim; in co-operative social societies in Norway and Sweden; and in barn-raisings, communes, and co-housing in the United States.

A few of my most memorable hands-on building experiences took place in central New Jersey, building wooden forts with the neighborhood kids; in New England, constructing a professor's innovative solar home with other students and the teacher; on a Greek island, crafting stone and stucco guest cottages with locals; and in southern California, helping to make a bamboo shade structure for a garden overlooking the Oceana Pacifica.

The word is spreading about bamboo. Bamboo's voice is getting louder and people are listening attentively. They are asking more and more questions. It is my hope that *Bamboo Style* has answered some of them and inspired new ones to be asked.

Sourcebook

Organizations

Represented here are various organizations in the USA and internationally that embody the global rhizomatic bamboo connections. I recommend starting with the Websites **www.americanbamboo.org** and **www.shakuhachi.com** for a comprehensive listing and direct Internet linkages—simplifying searching in the virtual reality of cyberspace.

USA

American Bamboo Society (ABS)
750 Krumkill Rd.
Albany, NY 12203-5976
518.458.7617
518.458.7625 fax
www.americanbamboo.org
The American Bamboo Society (ABS) is a nonprofit organization with regional chapters and worldwide membership that functions as the primary information source on bamboo in the USA. ABS publishes an extensive annual plant and product source list, a bimonthly news magazine, and an annual scientific journal. ABS sponsors an annual conference. Regional chapters publish newsletters and host workshops, presentations, bamboo festivals, and plant and product auctions. The ABS Website is an invaluable resource.

Earth Advocates Research Farm (EARF)
30 Myers Rd.
Summertown, TN 38483-7323
931.964.4151
www.thefarm.org/businesses/bamboo/tbq.html
EARF is a nonprofit dedicated to several bamboo-related ventures: performance trials of hardy bamboos in display gardens and groves; publishing the illustrated journal Temperate Bamboo Quarterly *(TBQ); classes, workshops, and short courses offered at their "Bamboo Institute of Tennessee." Can provide speakers on any aspect of Bamboo. EARF wholesales bamboos at "Our Bamboo Nursery" (see Nurseries) and is a certified Bamboo import/quarantine station. EARF maintains an extensive Bamboo library, welcomes researchers, and has an intern program available. Visits by appointment only.*

Pacific Bamboo Council
P.O. Box 454
Pahoa, HI 96778-0454
808.965.7182
Pacific Bamboo Council is a "nonprofit group of growers, artists, and craftspeople who promote the use and awareness of bamboo in the USA." (See ABS Website).

International

Environmental Bamboo Foundation (EBF)
P.O. Box 196
Ubud 80571
Bali, Indonesia
62.361.974.027
62.361.974.029 fax
www.bamboocentral.org
Founded by Linda Garland " . . . to incorporate a multidisciplinary approach to developing bamboo as an environmentally renewable non-wood forest resource." (See EBF or ABS Website) Develops educational programs and funding support through nonprofit arm—the International Bamboo Foundation (IBF). Medicinal uses information: www.bamboocentral.org/pharmacopoeia

EBF-Netherlands
info@ebf-bamboo.org

European Bamboo Society (EBS)
www.bodley.ox.ac.uk
EBS is ". . . an informal federation of national European bamboo societies, each of which has its own administration and membership." (See EBS Website) Convenes an annual meeting whose location is rotated amongst participating countries: Belgium, France, Germany, Great Britain, Netherlands, and Switzerland.

International Bamboo Association (IBA)
www.bamboo.org.au/iba/organization.htm
IBA ". . . helps facilitate, coordinate, and expand activities among regional bamboo societies and related organizations, and to encourage the formation of new bamboo societies in areas where bamboo is naturally prevalent." (See IBA Website)

IBA coordinates with INBAR in organizing and promoting World Bamboo Congress events held every 3 years. (Bali, Indonesia-1995; San Jose, Costa Rica-1998; upcoming: twice postponed due to devastating Indian earthquake in 2001 and 9/11/2001—in Debra Dun, India-2002)

International Development Research Center (IDRC)
Tanglin P.O. Box 101
Singapore 9124
Republic of Singapore
www.idrc.ca (Canada)
www.idrc.org.sg (Singapore)
IDRC is a source for an annotated bibliography "Bamboo as an Engineering Material."

International Network of Bamboo & Rattan (INBAR)
Anyuan Building No. 10, Anhui Beili,
Asian Games Village
Chaoyang District
Beijing 100101-80
Peoples Republic of China
86.10.649.56961
86.10.649.56983 fax
www.inbar.org.cn
INBAR ". . . develops and assists in the transfer of appropriate technologies and solutions to benefit the peoples of the world and their environment." (See INBAR Website.) INBAR publishes books, World Congress proceedings, and reports about bamboo and rattan.

Internet Connections

Arbors to Zithers List
http://kaui.net/bambooweb/bambooa2z.html

Bamboo Crafts eGroup
(Yahoo eGroup)
To join: http://groups.yahoo.com/group/bamboocrafts/join; or bamboocrafts-subscribe@yahoogroups.com
email: text (leave blank)
Informative discussion group and craft-related pictures posted.

Bamboo Crafts in America
(Sponsored by Northeast Chapter ABS)
www.northeastbamboo.org/crafts.cfm
To join/email: info@northeastbamboo.org
subject: JOIN CRAFTS LIST
Information related to bamboo crafts from events to construction tips.

Bamboo Plantations eGroup
(Yahoo eGroup)
www.egroups.com/group/bamboo-plantations
To join/email: bamboo-plantations-subscribe@egroups.com
text: leave blank
Informative discussion group focused on many aspects of growing bamboo.

Bamboo & Rattan Science and Technology Link (BARSTOOL)
To join: www.inbar.int/groups.htm

Consultative Groups on Bamboo & Rattan (CGBAR)
To join: www.inbar.int/groups.htm

Internet Bamboo Group (IBG)
Sponsored by the American Bamboo Society
bamboo@home.ease.lsoft.com
To Subscribe: listserve@home.ease.lsoft.com
Subject line: Blank
Text: SUBSCRIBE BAMBOO, First and Last Name
Archives Website: http://home.ease.lsoft.com/archives/bamboo.html
IBG is a forum for discussion of bamboo-related topics that has worldwide participation.

Workshops and Education

Hands-on workshops are conducted by practiced professional craftspersons. Participants are taught to work with bamboo—cutting, splitting, connecting—and learn techniques and use of tools. Regional ABS chapters, alternative building institutes, colleges, and universities periodically sponsor workshops.

Bamboo Branch
(See Fine Artists & Craftspersons)

Bamboo-Smiths
Doug and Martha Lingen, Reed Hamilton
P.O. Box 1801
Nevada City, CA 95959
530.292.9449
530.292.9460 fax
tbs@sierratimberframers.com

Bamboo Craftsman Co.
Troy Susan
2819 N. Winchell
Portland, OR 97217
503.285.5339
www.bamboocraftsman.com

Darrel DeBoer, Architect
1835 Pacific Ave.
Alameda, CA 94501
510.865.3669
510.865.7022 fax
DDarrelD@aol.com

Earth Advocates Research Farm
(See Organizations)
Adam and Sue Turtle

Rhode Island School of Design Bamboo Initiative
Michael McDonough, cofounder
Two College St.
Providence, RI 02903
401.454.6100
www.risd.edu
www.michaelmcdonough.com

Designers

The designers listed here have all participated in the creation of this book.

Architects

USA

Blackbird Architects
235 Palm Ave.
Santa Barbara, CA 93101
805.957.1315
805.957.1317 fax
www.bbird.com
Ken Radtkey and his firm design sustainable, "green" building projects, including their own offices.

Darrel DeBoer, Architect
(See Workshops)
Darrel is a renaissance professional and bamboo expert extraordinaire. He is a major force in promoting the possibilities of building with bamboo and has traveled from China to Colombia. He is a popular featured speaker at bamboo conferences and festivals. He designs with bamboo, grows bamboo, teaches about bamboo, speaks about bamboo, and writes about bamboo. He instructs bamboo-lovers in his workshops and together they build garden shade structures, footbridge trusses, and learn how to build a scale model of their own designs using bamboo skewers and a hot glue gun. He also is an alternative construction designer using a "green" approach. His designs have included a "strawbale-and-bamboo truss" retreat and a dwelling with bamboo strawbale reinforcement. He is a published author, is written about, and writes for magazines.

He designed, described, photographed, carved, and crafted the pen, ladle, and vase container in the "On Your Own" chapter.

Eco Architects
David Sands, Architect
P.O. Box 868
Paia, HI 96779
808.572.3033
808.572.2146 fax
www.bamboohardwoods.com
bamboo@maui.net
David designs bamboo dwellings that are built by Bamboo Technologies with materials primarily sourced through Bamboo Hardwoods. He is very active in material lab testing of bamboo for building-code recognition internationally.

Fernau Hartman Architects
Richard Fernau, Architect
Laura Hartman, Architect
2512 9th St. #2
Berkeley, CA 94710
510.848.4480
510.848.4532 fax
www.fernauhartman.com
Richard Fernau designed a bamboo tree house that includes a bamboo ladder and a bamboo framework.

GBG Architect
Gale Beth Goldberg, AIA, NCARB
322 Elizabeth St.
Santa Barbara, CA 93103
805.966.9038 tel/fax
http://home.earthlink.net/~montecito/
(Iron Grass, Vegetable Steel)
www.gibbs-smith.com
montecito@earthlink.net
Gale is passionate about building with bamboo and living with bamboo indoors and outdoors. She researches, writes, and gives presentations about bamboo. She has traveled from

Bali to Colombia to study bamboo construction, and received funding from the Graham Foundation for Advanced Studies in the Fine Arts to support her research and documentation, "Iron Grass, Vegetable Steel," about the bamboo architecture of Simón Vélez and Marcelo Villegas. Her architectural design projects incorporate bamboo in many modalities, including living bamboo, harvested bamboo, and bamboo arts and crafts.

Kirk Gradin, Architect
630 Garden St.
Santa Barbara, CA 93101
805.564.4423
805.564.2678 fax
kirk@d4s.net
Kirk designed his own home remodel with bamboo on the floor, as the cabinets, as part of a wall fountain, and in several furniture pieces of his design. His interior bamboo architecture includes both stylish bamboo furniture and antiques.

RPM Architects
Robert Peale Mehl, Architect
3568 Sagunto
Santa Ynez, CA 93460
805.688.7281
805.688.5902
rpm@syv.com
RPM Architects are "green" building designers who use a holistic approach to create projects from wineries to residences using straw bale, adobe, and other innovative materials.

Michael McDonough, Architect
www.michaelmcdonough.com
Michael is an innovative designer of and teacher about modern bamboo furniture and bamboo as a building material.

Thompson-Naylor Architects
L. Dennis Thompson, Architect
900 Philinda Ave.
Santa Barbara, CA 93103
805.966.9807
805.966.2309 fax
www.silcom.com/~tna
Thompson-Naylor Architects designs sustainable "green" projects ranging from residences to religious structures.

International

McKinley Dang Burkhart Design Group
Walker McKinley, Architect
805-A 17th Ave. SW
Calgary, Alberta
Canada
403.229.2037
403.229.2517 fax
www.mdbworld.com
Walker McKinley designed several restaurants incorporating harvested bamboo in the interior decor.

Simón Vélez, Architect
Bogota, Colombia
011.57.1.34.10.323
011.57.1.34.28.147 fax
Simón, who calls himself a "roof architect," has pioneered the design of large constructions that are built with bamboo in Colombia and internationally. He is recognized as an innovative architect and has presented his work at several World Congresses on Bamboo and participated in bamboo building workshops in the Americas and Europe. He is a published author, and has had numerous articles and a book published about his bamboo architecture.

Interior Designers

Barbara Farish
Santa Barbara, CA 93111
805.969.1512
Barbara's interior designs include tropical island vacation style translated into daily living.

Sue Firestone Associates
Sue Firestone, designer
5383 Hollister Ave., Ste. 140
Santa Barbara, CA 93111
805.692.1948
805.692.9293 fax
www.sfadesign.com
Sue and her associates design interior environments with sophisticated bamboo furniture and furnishings.

Linda Garland
Interior Design
P.O. Box 196
Ubud, Bali, Indonesia
62.361.974.028
62.361.974.029 fax
www.lindagarland.com
linda@denpasar.wasantara.net.id
Linda's sophisticated and innovative bamboo furniture designs and bamboo architectural interiors are found from the islands of Indonesia and the Pacific to the Caribbean.

Corinna Gordon
Interior Design
1155 Coast Village Rd.
Montecito, CA 93108
805.565.1593
805.565.5363 fax
www.corinnagordon.com
Corinna creates a distinctive elegance in her interior design projects located worldwide using stylish and sophisticated bamboo furniture and furnishings. Contemporary and antique styles are blended with original designs of bamboo furnishings.

**Jessica Helgerson
Interior Design**
232 Anacapa St., Ste. 2C
Santa Barbara, CA 93101
805.560.0691
805.560.0781 fax
www.jhinteriordesign.com
Jessica and her associates design environmentally sustainable "green" interior projects that include antique and contemporary bamboo furniture, furnishings, and accessories alongside other natural and recycled materials.

**Ann James
Interior Design**
611 Orchard Ave.
Montecito, CA 93108
805.969.4554
anniej93108@yahoo.com
Ann designs wonderfully elegant interiors with a panache that is highlighted in her choice of antique and modern bamboo furniture, contemporary bamboo furnishings, objects, and accessories.

Korpinen & Erickson Design Associates
Neil Korpinen, Eric Erickson, designers
2496 Lillie Ave.
Summerland, CA 93067
805.565.0303
805.565.0203 fax
k-einc@home.com
Neil and Eric design tropical interior decors with bamboo furniture, finishes, and accessories.

Maienza Limited
John Maienza, Architect
29 E. Victoria St.
Santa Barbara, CA 93101
805.966.5010
805.966.7366 fax
www.inthegarden.com/jmaienza.htm
design@johnmaienza.com
John designs interiors with stylish bamboo furniture and furnishings.

Christopher Teasley Interior Design
1187 Coast Village Rd., Ste. 9
Montecito, CA 93108
805.969.4005
805.969.6345 fax
Christopher and his associates design sophisticated interiors with high-end bamboo furniture, furnishings, and finishes.

TK Designs
Carpinteria, CA
805.684.2654
tbamboo@silcom.com

TK designs residential projects with bamboo furniture and furnishings, both modern and antique.

Landscape Architects and Horticulturists

Susanne Lucas
Horticulturist
9 Bloody Pond Rd.
Plymouth, MA 02360
508.224.7982
susannelucas@adelphia.net
Susanne is an avid bamboo enthusiast who serves as president of the American Bamboo Society, designs with bamboo, consults on bamboo plantings, and gives presentations internationally.

Michael Van Valkenburgh Associates Inc.
Landscape Architects
231 Concord Ave.
Cambridge, MA 02138
617.864.2076
617.492.3128 fax
www.mvvainc.com
mvva_ma@mvvainc.com
Michael and his firm design landscapes with bamboo plantings.

Van Atta Associates, Landscape Architecture
Susan Van Atta, Landscape Architect
235 Palm Ave.
Santa Barbara, CA 93101
805.730.7444
805.730.7446 fax
www.silcom.com/~vanattap
Susan Van Atta and her firm are sustainable activists and designers who, along with Blackbird Architects, designed their very "green" offices, including bamboo cabinetry and flooring.

Fine Artists and Craftspersons

Nancy Moore Bess
186 Harkness Rd.
Amherst, MA 01002
413.253.0459
413.253.0458 fax
nancybess@aol.com
Nancy's work as an internationally recognized basket weaver integrates bamboo with natural woven textile fibers. She is a published author and a delightful, captivating, and accomplished speaker, presenting the uses of bamboo in Japan and in her own creations.

Charissa Brock
503.358.4222
www.firebright.com/brock/
charissa_brock@hotmail.com
Charissa's sculptures use bamboo in harmony with other natural fibers, woods, and stones.

Gary Chafe
P.O. Box 2134
Santa Barbara, CA 93102
805.963.3551
www.garychafe.com
grchafe@hotmail.com
Gary is an accomplished artist who works in several mediums and has recently incorporated bamboo into his design expressions.

Dorothy Churchill-Johnson
125 C North Milpas St.
Santa Barbara, CA 93103
805.966.6561
Dorothy depicts bamboo in her carefully detailed and alive acrylic and oil canvases.

James Clever
(See Outdoor Applications-Poles)
James crafts bamboo-motif jewelry in sterling silver.

Hazel Beatrice Colditz
3302 E. Linden St.
Tucson, AZ 85716
520.319.9882
520.320.3711 fax
isoldehaze@aol.com
Hazel's bamboo motif is expressed through her welded metal-tube compositions.

Shari Arai DeBoer
1835 Pacific Ave.
Alameda, CA 94501
510.865.3669
shari_deboer@yahoo.com
Shari's artistic watercolors depict living bamboo in groves and together with other flowering vines.

Stephen Glassman
(See Marketplace: Outdoor Applications—Bridges & Site Sculpture)
Stephen works with bamboo in a sculptural and site-specific mode, creating functional expressions as well as public art experiences.

Mineko Grimmer
10747 Wilshire Blvd. #504
Los Angeles, CA 90024
310.470.9043
grimmerj@email.emerson.com

Mineko creates kinetic, experiential bamboo sculptural forests where she uses bamboo both visually and as a sound-producing element in her work.

Calvin Hashimoto, sculptor
P.O. Box 1274
Kealakekua, HI 96750
808.326.9894
www.bamboofinearts.com
bambooda@gte.net
Cal skillfully sculpts with bamboo to create freestanding and wall-hung contemporary art pieces that are an attempt to incorporate what he calls the "serenity, beauty, and spirituality of a bamboo forest" into his expressions.

Carol Malone and Mark Meckes
Bamboo Branch
6707 Willamette Dr.
Austin, TX 78723
512.929.9565
512.927.2127 fax
bamboo@texas.net
Carol and Mark create bamboo crafts, sell custom cut bamboo pieces for craft-making, and conduct craft workshops.

Beverly Ann Messenger
Santa Barbara, CA
805.683.6612
bamboomessengerwoman@earthlink.net
Beverly designs and crafts with bamboo, plays music with bamboo instruments, and composes bamboo poetry.

Gerard Minakawa
UKAO
309 Palm Ave, Ste B
Santa Barbara, CA 93101
805.963.6261
805.963.6271 fax
www.minakawastudios.com
design@minakawastudios.com
Gerard crafts bamboo into contemporary pergolas, fences, and furniture. He contributed the pergola plans featured in the "On Your Own" chapter.

Lynn Nakamura
634 N. Doheny Dr.
Los Angeles, CA 90069
310.205.0733
310.205.0730 fax
LTNLA@earthlink.net
Lynn designs exquisite jewelry created with finely crafted bamboo clasps and whole, bent-bamboo designs. She is also introducing unusual bamboo housewares.

Jill Vander Hoof
P.O. Box 50214
Santa Barbara, CA 93150
805.565.7134
805.565.7161 fax
Jill carves marble into creative sculptures that include a bamboo marble piece with culm sheaths attached, and these inter-nodal elements rotate about the main stalk.

Custom Builders and Constructors

USA

Bamboo Craftsman Co.
(See Outdoor Applications)
Troy Susan
Troy designs and builds custom bamboo structures for outdoors and indoors.

Bamboo Technologies
Jeffree Trudeau, construction project manager and builder
120 Hana Hwy #9
Paia, HI 96779
808.243.0112
808.573.1944 fax
www.bamboohardwoods.com
bamboo@maui.net
Jeffree, along with a team of constructors, build site-specific custom-designed bamboo structures. The company also manufactures prefabricated structures.

Bamboo Builders Northwest
PMB 234
4509 Interlake Ave. North
Seattle, WA 98103
206.789.1330
www.bamboobuilders.com
All types of outdoor structures and furniture are built by this company.

Ecoterrestrial Concepts
P. O. Box 461
Kurtistown, HI 96760
808.966.9062 tel/fax
ecoterre@interpac.net
Leimana Pelton builds with bamboo and is developing a building system that uses joinery and methods in the design of modulated movable structures that are suitable for inexperienced bamboo constructors.

Island Ambiance
(See Fences & Outdoor Structures)
Jo Scheer
Jo builds bamboo tree houses, furniture, and furnishings.

Thangmaker Construction
Frank Meyer
904 E. Monroe
Austin, TX 78704
512.282.2341 tel/fax
members.aol.com/
thangmaker/myhomepage/sl/
Builders of bamboo furniture and accessories.

International

Michel Abadie
14 Rue Brichart de Saron, 75009
Paris, France
33 1 4878 3305
bam@calva.net
Michel designs and builds bamboo airplanes—Flyboo.

Jörg Stamm
(See Marketplace-Bridges-International)

Marcelo Villegas
CRA 21 No. 72A-21
Manizales, Colombia
09 68 867 752
09 68 867 956 fax
Marcelo is a master builder and constructor of bamboo buildings, furniture, and furnishings. He works on his own projects and in collaboration with Simón Vélez.

Bamboo Nurseries

USA

Author's Note: Nurseries listed are either ones I am directly familiar with or represent geographical diversity.

For additional nursery listings in your area, refer to the **American Bamboo Society** Source List.

All listings sell retail unless noted otherwise.

California

Bamboo Bob's Pura Vida
1541 Sunset Dr.
Vista, CA 92083
760.726.4038
bamboobob@home.com

Bamboo Giant Nursery
5601 Freedom Blvd.
Aptos, CA 95003
831.687.0100
831.687.0200 fax
www.bamboogiant.com

Bamboo Sourcery
666 Wagnon Rd.
Sebastopol, CA 95472
707.823.5866
707.829.8106 fax
www.bamboosourcery.com

Endangered Species
23280 Stephanie
Perris, CA 92570
800.709.5568
909.943.0990
909.943.9199 fax
www.endangeredspecies.com
Wholesale.

San Marcos Growers
125 S. San Marcos Rd.
Santa Barbara, CA 93160
805.683.1565
805.964.1329 fax
www.smgrowers.com
Wholesale.

Pacific Northwest

Bamboo Craftsman Co.
(See Outdoor Applications - Poles)

Bamboo Garden
1507 SE Alder
Portland, OR 97214
503.654.0024
503.231.9387 fax
www.bamboogarden.com
Retail and wholesale.

Bamboo Gardener
(See Outdoor Applications - Poles)

Bamboo Guy
6005 Weber Rd.
Tillamook, OR 97141
503.842.7329
www.bambooguy.com

Beauty and the Bamboo Co.
306 NW 84th St.
Seattle, WA 98117
206.781.9790
206.297.2810 fax
bambu501@aol.com
Retail and wholesale.

Tradewinds Bamboo Nursery
28446 Hunter Creek Loop
Gold Beach, OR 97444
541.247.0835 tel/fax
www.bamboodirect.com

Hawaii

Hale Ohe Ltd.
P.O. Box 107
Hakalau, HI 96710
808.963.6882 tel/fax
bamboos@gte.net

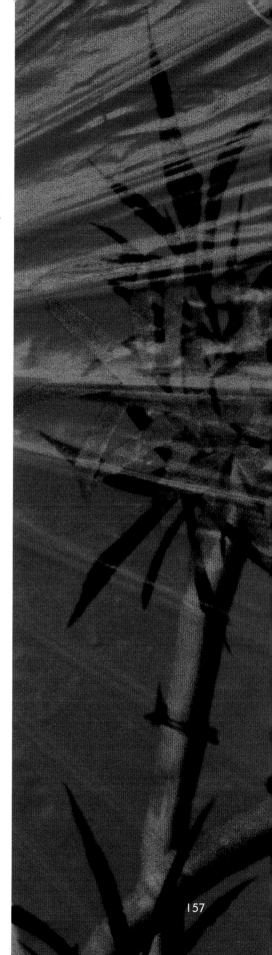

Quindembo Bamboo Nursery
P.O. Box 44556
Kawaihae, HI 96743
808.885.4975 fax
www.bamboonursery.com
Retail and wholesale.

Southwest

Bamboo Ranch
Tucson, AZ 85745
520.743.9879 tel/fax
bamboo@azstarnet.com
Retail and wholesale.

West

Horticultural Consultants Inc.
5300 N. Braeswood, PMB 382
Houston, TX 77096
713.665.7256
713.665.0565 fax
www.horticulturalconsultantsinc.com
Wholesale.

**Wild Screwbean Utility
Residential Garden**
638 Tillery St.
Austin, TX 78702
512.386.9453
512.386.9455 fax
www.bambootexas.com
Retail and wholesale.

Midwest

Burton's Bamboo Garden
7352 Gheils Carrol Rd.
Morrow, OH 45152
513.899.3446
www.burtonsbamboogarden.com

Southeast

Bamboo Gardens of Louisiana
38124 Hwy. 440
Mt. Hermon, LA 70450
985.795.2300
985.795.8300 fax
www.mosobamboo.com
Retail and wholesale.

Bambooscape
Miami, FL
305.662.2315
305.669.6842 fax
bambooscape@aol.com

Hollow Bamboo
498 Keel Hollow Rd.
New Hope, AL 35760
256.723.4960
hollowbamboo@yahoo.com
Retail and wholesale.

jmbamboo
4176 Humber Rd.
Dora, AL 35062
205.648.3998
www.jmbamboo.com

Lewis Bamboo Groves
265 Creekview Rd.
Oakman, AL 35579
205.686.5728 tel/fax
www.lewisbamboo.com

Linton & Linton Bamboo
310 Woodbine Rd.
Savannah, GA 31410
912.897.5755
912.897.9935 fax
www.LLBamboo.com
Retail and wholesale.

Morningside Gardens & Nursery
1170 Hwy 64
Morrilton, AR 72110
501.354.8470 tel/fax
Retail and wholesale.

Ozark Bamboo Garden
1059 CR 266
Eureka Springs, AR 72631
501.253.6801 tel/fax
bamboos@cswnet.com

Tornello Nursery
P.O. Box 789
Ruskin, FL 33570
813.645.5445
813.645.4353 fax
www.tornellobamboo.com
*Wholesale supplier of containerized
bamboo.*

Tropical Bamboo
4871 NW 15th St.
Coconut Creek, FL 33063
954.975.9500
www.tropicalbamboo.com
Retail and wolesale.

Mid Atlantic

David Day
13816 Lawyers Rd.
Charlotte, NC 28227
704.545.0141

Kalakirya Howff
5879 Breckinridge Mill Rd.
Fincastle, VA 24090
540.992.5793
littltn@rbnet.com

Lone Oak Farm
2219 Neeley's Bend Rd.
Madison, TN 37115
615.865.9933 tel/fax
www.loneoakfarm-bamboo.com
Retail and wholesale.

Mid Atlantic Bamboo
1458 Dusty Rd.
Crewe, VA 23930
804.645.7662
www.midatlanticbamboo.com

Our Bamboo Nursery
30 Myers Rd.
Summertown, TN 38483
931.964.4151
931.964.4228 fax
www.growit.com/bamboo
Retail and wholesale.

Robin Williams
906 W. Outer Dr.
Oak Ridge, TN 37830
865.482.2908
Retail and wholesale.

Atlantic

Asian Influence
303 Casino Dr.
Farmingdale, NJ 07727
732.938.4775
732.751.1220 fax
tpalven@worldnet.att.net

David C. Andrews
P.O. Box 358
Oxon Hill, MD 20750
bambubambu@aol.com

East-West Bamboo Farm and Nursery
14 Yellow City Rd.
Amenia, NY 12501
845.373.9020
845.373.5788 fax
Doloresbo3@aol.com
Retail and wholesale.

Hampton Grass and Bamboo Inc.
P.O. Box 2522
Southhampton, NY 11969
631.725.8499 tel/fax
HamptonsGrass@aol.com

Landscapes Plus
P.O. Box 156
Pluckemin, NJ 07908
908.658.3055

Little Acre Farm
223 Victory Rd.
Howell, NJ 07731
732.938.6300
732.938.6340 fax
www.littleacrefarm.com
Retail and wholesale.

Oriental Garden Supply
23 Great Oak Ln.
Pittsford, NY 14534
716.586.4969
716.586.8945 fax
www.OrientalGardenSupply.com

Upper Bank Nurseries
P.O. Box 486
Media, PA 19063
610.566.0679
Retail and wholesale.

Northeast

New England Bamboo Co.
5 Granite St.
Rockport, MA 01966
978.546.3581
978.546.1075 fax
www.newenglandbamboo.com
Retail and wholesale.

Tripple Brook Farm
37 Middle Rd.
Southampton, MA 01073
413.527.4626
413.527.9853 fax
www.tripplebrookfarm.com
Retail and wholesale.

International

Australia

Bamboo Australia
1171 Kenilworth Rd.
Belli Park, Queensland
Australia 4562
61.07.5447.0299
www.bamboo-oz.com.au

Bamboo Land
7 Old Coach Rd.
Howard 4659 Queensland
Australia
61.07.4129.4470
61.07.4129.0130 fax
www.satcom.net.au/bambooland

Earthcare Enterprises
P.O. Box 500
Maleny, Queensland 4552
Australia
61.07.5494.4666
www.earthcare.com.au

Canada

Canada's Bamboo World
Box 71025
#125-8115 120 St.
Delta, B.C. V4C 8E6
Canada
604.596.2090
604.596.0507 fax
www.bambooworld.com
Retail and wholesale.

The Plant Farm
177 Vesuvius Bay Rd.
Salt Spring Island, BC V8K 1K3
Canada
250.537.5995 tel/fax
http://theplantfarm.ca
Retail and wholesale.

China

China Bamboo Centre
(Yunnan Province)
www.chinabamboocentre.com

Yunfeng Gardens
Rm 4048, 4F
Guanfeng Mansion
South St.
Houzou, Zhejiang, China.
86.572.205.8027
86.572.203.3877 fax
www.yunfeng-gardens.com.cn

France

La Bambouseraie de Prafrance
30140 Generargue
Anduze, France
04.66.61.78.80
(commercial export)
www.bambouseraie.fr
Retail and to professionals.

Germany

Bambus-Centrum Deutschland
Saarstrasse 3
D - 76532
Baden-Baden, Germany
0049.7221.50740
0049.7221.50748 fax
www.bambus.de

Ireland

Stam's Bamboo Nursery Ltd.
www.stambamboo.com

Japan

Takehei Bamboo Corp.
43 Omiya-gojo
Shimogyo-ku
Kyoto, Japan 600-8377
81.75.801.6453
81.75.802.6277 fax
www.takkehei.jp

Netherlands

Bamboekwerkerij Fastuosa
www.users.bart.nl/~jkerfast

Places to Visit

USA

California

**Bamboo Garden—
Japanese Cultural Center**
Foothill College
12345 El Monte Rd.
Los Altos, CA 94022
408.255.4085
www.bamboogarden.org

Hakone Japanese Gardens
21000 Big Basin Way
Saratoga, CA 95070
408.741.4994
www.hakone.com

**Huntington Library, Art
Collections, and Botanical
Gardens**
1151 Oxford Rd.
San Marino, CA 91108
626.405.2100
www.huntington.org

**Japanese-American Cultural and
Community Center**
244 S. Pedro St.
Los Angeles, CA 90012
213.628.2725
213.617.8576 fax
www.jacc.org

Japanese Tea Garden
Hagiwara Tea Garden Dr.
Golden Gate Park
San Francisco, CA 94117
415.752.1171
www.gardenforum.com/
japanese_tea_garden.html

Los Angeles Arboretum
301 N. Baldwin Ave.
Arcadia, CA 91007
626.821.3222
www.arboretum.org

**Los Angeles City Japanese
Garden**
6100 Woodley Ave.
Van Nuys, CA 91406
818.756.8166
www.ci.la.ca.us/
SAN/sanjgad.htm

Lotusland
695 Ashley Rd.
Montecito, CA 93108
805.969.9990
www.lotusland.org

San Diego Zoo
Giant Panda Research Station
Balboa Park
San Diego, CA 92101
619.231.1515
www.sandiegoattraction.com/
sandiegozoo.html

**Strybing Arboretum and
Botanical Gardens**
9th Ave. at Lincoln Way
Golden Gate Park
San Francisco, CA 94122
415.661.1316
www.strybing.org

Quail Botanical Gardens
230 Quail Gardens Dr.
Encinitas, CA 92042
760.436.3036
760.632.0917 fax
www.qbgardens.com

Pacific Northwest

Japanese Garden
611 SW Kingston Ave.
Portland, OR 97201
503.223.1321
503.223.8303 fax
www.japanesegarden.com

**Portland Classical Chinese
Garden**
Garden of Awakening Orchids
NW 3rd and Everett
Portland, OR 97208
503.228.8131
www.chinesegarden.org

Woodland Park Zoo
5500 Phinney Ave.
N. Seattle, WA 98103
206.684.4800
www.woodland-park-zoo.visit-
seattle.com

Midwest

Zilker Botanical Gardens
2220 Barton Springs Rd.
Austin, TX 78746
512.477.8672
www.zilker-garden.org

Southeast

Atlanta Botanical Gardens
1345 Piedmont Ave.
Atlanta, GA 30309
404.876.5859
www.atlantabotanicalgarden.org

**Bamboo Farm and Coastal
Gardens**
University of Georgia
College of Agriculture and
Environmental Sciences
2 Canebrake Rd.
Savannah, GA 31419
912.921.5460
www.ces.uga.edu

Birmingham Botanical Gardens
2612 Lane Park Rd.
Birmingham, AL 35223
205.414.3950
www.bbgardens.org

Fairchild Botanical Gardens
10901 Old Cutter Rd.
Coral Gables, FL 33156
305.667.1651
www.fbg.org

Jungle Gardens Avery Island
Avery Island, LA 70513
www.tabasco.com

Kanapaha Botanical Gardens
4700 SW 58th Dr.
Gainesville, FL 32608
904.372.4981
www.hammock.ifas.ufl.edu

Leu Gardens
1920 N. Forest Ave.
Orlando, FL 32903
407.246.2620
www.leugardens.org

Marie Selby Botanical Gardens
811 S. Palm Ave.
Sarasota, FL 34236
941.366.5731
www.selby.org

Morikami Museum & Gardens
Morikami Park Rd.
Delray Beach, FL 33446
561.495.0233
www.morikami.org

Mid-Atlantic

Biltmore Estate
One North Pack Square
Asheville, NC 28801
800.624.1575
www.biltmore.com

**Cheekwood Botanical Gardens
and Museum of Art**
1200 Forrest Park Dr.
Nashville, TN 37205
615.356.8000
www.cheekwood.org

**Lewis Ginter Botanical
Gardens**
1800 Lakeside Ave.
Richmond, VA 23228
804.262.9887
www.lewisginter.org

Maymont Foundation-Gardens
1700 Hampton St.
Richmond, VA 23220
804.358.7166
www.maymont.org

National Zoo
40 Massachusetts Ave. NE
Washington, D.C. 20002
202.216.9073
www.natzoo.si.edu

**North Carolina Zoological
Park**
4401 Zoo Parkway
Asheboro, NC 27203
800.488.0444
www.nczoo.org

Atlantic

Brooklyn Botanical Gardens
1000 Washington Ave.
Brooklyn, NY 11225
718.623.7200
wwwbbg.org

Longhouse Reserve
133 Hands Creek Rd.
East Hampton, NY 11937
631.329.3568
www.longhouse.org

New York Botanical Gardens
Bronx River Parkway at
Fordham Rd.
Bronx, NY 10458
718.817.8700
www.bbg.org

Willowood Arboretum
170 Longview Rd.
Chester, NJ 07930
973.326.7600
www.state.nj.us

Northeast

Arnold Arboretum
Arborway
Jamaica Plain, MA 02130
617.524.1717
www.arboretum.harvard.edu

Tower Hill Botanical Gardens
11 French Dr.
West Boylston, MA 01505
508.869.6111
www.towerhillbg.org

International

China

**The Bamboo Forest of South
Sichuan**
www.scti.ac.cn

France

La Bambouseraie de Prafrance
(See Nurseries-International)

La Bambouseraie de Lériet
(near Toulouse)
www.members.aol.com/
LerietBamboo

Germany

Bambus-Centrum Deutschland
(See Nurseries-International)

Great Britain

Carwinion Gardens
Carwinion Rd.
Mawnan Smith
Falmouth
01.326.250.258
www.gardensincorwal.co.uk/
carwinion/carwinion.htm

**The Royal
Botanical Gardens at Kew**
Richmond, Surrey
London
England TW9 3AB
020.8940.1171
www.rbgkew.org.uk

Japan

The Bamboo Museum
Rakusai Bamboo Park
Kyoto, Japan
81.75.331.3821
www.isei.or.jp/
Bamboo_Museum/
Bamboo_Museum.html

The companies and people listed in the Marketplace are just a beginning of your bamboo purchasing options. Here you will find national and international sources for furniture, furnishings, flooring, accessories, poles and plants. Have fun exploring your own region and the planet, all the while discovering bamboo treasures.

Sources that I can personally recommend through experience are marked with a red asterisk *.

The term "to the Trade" means that only professional designers may order.

To explore further, my recommendation is to search the Internet—a fantastic, and sometimes overwhelming, rhizomatic network of all things bamboo—which can lead to bamboo adventures that are beyond your wildest dreams. Just enter "bamboo furniture" and see what you find. Specificity in surfing (on a bamboo surfboard—check it out at www.bamboosurfboards.com.au or www.goodtime.com.au) the "Bamboo Web" will help focus your results.

Indoor Applications

Furniture Manufacturers and Retailers

USA

Bamboo Mountain Imports
2240-B 4th St.
San Rafael, CA 94901
707.944.8489
707.944.0488 fax
www.bamboomountain.com
Furniture manufacturer; retail.

Big Bamboo Warehouse
400 Hana Hwy #E
Kahului, Maui, HI 96732
808.877.4141
808.877.4151 fax
www.bigbamboomaui.com
Stylish furniture; retail.

* **Celadon House**
1220 State St.
Santa Barbara, CA 93101
805.899.4676
805.899.4576 fax www.celadonhouse.com
Teak and bamboo furniture; retail.

French Country Living
10135 Colvin Run Rd.
Great Falls, VA 22066
800.485.1302
703.759.2245 fax
www.frenchcountry.com
Stylish furniture; retail.

Richard Gervais Collection
965 Natoma Street
San Francisco, CA 94103
415.255.4579
415.255.0453 fax
www.richardgervaiscollection.com
Asian antiques retail; to the Trade.

* **Island Ambiance**
459 Normal Ave.
Ashland, OR 97520
541.482.6357
http://netdial.caribe.net~bamboo
Stylish furniture.

* **Kim 3**
1117 State St.
Santa Barbara, CA 93101
805.966.0989
805.966.0931 fax
www.kim3.com
High-end sophisticated furniture; retail.

* **Linda Garland**
P.O. Box 196
Ubud, Bali, Indonesia
62.361.974028
62.361.974029 fax
www.lindagarland.com
Sophisticated furniture.

* **William Laman**
1496 E. Valley Rd.
Montecito, CA 93108
805.969.2840
805.969.2839 fax
www.williamlaman.com
Sophisticated furniture; retail.

* **Michael McDonough Architect**
www.michaelmcdonough.com
High-tech laminated furniture; retail.

* **McGuire Furniture Company**
1201 Bryant St.
San Francisco, CA 94103
800.662.4847
www.mcguirefurniture.com
High-end sophisticated furniture; to the Trade.

Nancy Brous Associates
1008 Lexington Ave.
New York, NY 10021
212.772.7515
212.753.9587 fax
High-end sophisticated furniture; retail.

Newel Art Galleries, Inc.
425 East 53rd St
New York, NY 10022
212.758.1970
212.371.0166 fax
www.newel.com
Victorian bamboo furniture

Objects Plus, Inc.
315 E. 62nd St., 3rd floor
New York, NY 10021
212.832.3386
High-end sophisticated furniture; retail.

One Beach Rd.
1118 State St.
Santa Barbara, CA 93101
805.962.9379
805.962.5250 fax
www.onebeachrd.com
Stylish furniture; retail.

* **Pier 1 Imports**
P.O. Box 961020
Fort Worth, TX 96161-0020
800.447.4371
817.252.8841 fax
www.pier1.com
Stylish furniture; retail.

Pierce Martin
ADAC West, Ste. B-2
349 Peachtree Hills Rd.
Atlanta, GA 30305
800.334.8701
404.872.0859 fax
www.piercemartin.com
Stylish furniture; to the Trade.

Simply Bamboo
P.O. Box 858
Durham, CA 95938
800.587.4746
530.345.5292
www.simplybamboo.com
Stylish Chinese furniture; retail.

The Bombay Company
P.O. Box 161009
Fort Worth, TX 76161-1009
800.829.7789
www.bombayco.com
Stylish furniture; retail.

* **The Budji Collections, Inc.**
1024 Briggs Hwy
Rising Sun, MD 21911
410.658.3126
410.658.3758 fax
www.budji.com
High-end sophisticated furniture; to the Trade.

The Plantation Shop
3193 Roswell Rd.
Atlanta, GA 30305
888.879.2486
404.239.1866 fax
www.theplantationshop.com
Stylish furniture; retail.

* **Yucatan Bamboo**
5 Woods Edge Ln.
Houston, TX 77024
713.278.7344
713.278.7355 fax
Yucabambu@aol.com
www.bamboofencer.com
Stylish furniture; retail.

International

* **Bamboofurniture.com.au**
Shop 3
10 Main St.
Palmwoods, Queensland, 4555,
Australia
07.547.883310
www.bamboofurniture.com.au
Stylish furniture; retail.

Bambù Design
Via Donatello, 37
Milano, Italy
39.02.7063688 tel/fax
www.bambudesign.it
Sophisticated furniture.

Brian Erickson
P.O. Box Apdo.295-7210
Guapiles - Pocici
Costa Rica, Central America
011.506.7010.1958
011.506.7010.2264 fax
brieri99@yahoo.com
www.earthcare.com.au/b_erickson.htm

Original Bamboo Factory
Caymanas Estates
Spanish P.O.
Jamaica, West Indies
809.933.2883 tel/fax
www originalbamboofactory.com
Stylish furniture; retail.

Weiming Furniture Ltd.
62 Bell Rd.
Sittingbourne, Kent
ME 10 4HE
United Kingdom
44.1795.472262
44.1795.422633 fax
www.weimingfurniture.com
Stylish furniture; retail.

Interior Finish Materials

USA

Bamboo Depot
393-D E. Channel Rd.
Benecia, CA 94510
888.273.6888
707.751.3898
707.751.0168 fax
www.bamboobridge.com
Paneling, mats, boards; retail/wholesale.

Bamboo & Rattan Works, Inc.
470 Oberlin Ave. S.
Lakewood, NJ 08701
800.422.6266
732.905.8386 fax
www.bambooandrattan.com
Reed matting; retail.

Bamboo Maui Inc.
P.O. Box 1758
Wailuku, HI 96793
808.244.2299
808.244.3378 fax
www.bamboomaui.com
Paneling, veneer; retail.

Bamboo Too
74-5598 Luhia St.
Kailua-Kona, HI 96740
808.322.5648 tel/fax
*Woven bamboo peel matting;
retail/wholesale.*

Benson's Import
15591 Container Ln.
Huntington Beach, CA 92649
714.893.3217
714.893.3056 fax
www.bensonsimport.com
Tropical decor; retail/wholesale.

Frank's Cane & Rush Supply
7252 Heil Ave.
Huntington Beach, CA 92647
714.847.0707
714.843.5645 fax
www.franksupply.com
Tropical decor; retail/wholesale.

* **Happy Horticulture**
2100 Meadow Vista Rd.
Meadow Vista, CA 95722
530.878.1035
530.878.9378 fax
www.happyhorticulture.com
Woven matting.

* **Smith & Fong-Plyboo**
(See Flooring)
Paneling, tambour, veneer.

Stark Wallcovering
979 3rd Ave.
New York, NY 10022
212.355.7186
212.753.3761 fax
www.starkcarpet.com
Bamboo motif wallpaper; to the Trade.

Yucatan Bamboo
(See Furniture)
Interior materials

International

Fence and Bamboo International Co. Ltd.
Rm 2604 Jin Ding Building
373 Long Kou Rd. West
Guangzhou, China
86.20.87582129 fax
www.bamboocane.com
Ceiling and wall coverings; retail exporter.

KandM Bamboo Products Inc.
300 Esna Park Dr., Unit 26
Markham ONT L3R 1H3
Canada
905.947.1688
905.947.1588 fax
www.myna.com/bamboo
Paneling.

Flooring

USA

Basically Bamboo
P.O. Box 177
Kamuela, HI 96743
808.885.7722
808.885.3431 fax
www.basicallybamboo.com
Flooring and "bamboards"; retail.

Bamboo Flooring Hawaii
Foreign Trade Zone # 9
521 Ala Moana Blvd., Ste. 213
Honolulu, HI 96814
877.502.2626
808.505.8090 fax
www.bambooflooringhawaii.com
Retail/wholesale.

Bamboo Flooring International
10950 Currier Rd.
Walnut Creek, CA 91789
800.827.9261
www.bamboo-flooring.com
Retail/wholesale.

Bamboo Hardwoods, Inc.
6402 Roosevelt Way NE
Seattle, WA 98115
206.264.2414
206.264.9365 fax
www.bamboohardwoods.com
Retail/wholesale.

California Bamboo Flooring Co.
Tan-Pri Int'l Inc.
888.548.7548
www.californiabamboo.com
Retail.

D & M Bamboo Flooring Company
858 Sivert Dr.
Wood Dale, IL 60191
630.860.2009
630.860.3803 fax
www.dmbamboo.com
"Eco-Wood"; retail/wholesale.

Luna Bambu Inc.
133 NW 94th St.
Miami Shores, FL 33150
lunabambu@earthlink.net
Retail.

Mintec Corp.
100 E. Pennsylvania Ave.
Townson, MD 21286
888.964.6832
410.296.6688
410.296.6693 fax
www.bamtex.com
"Bamtex," retail/wholesale.

Moso.com
800.617.2324
800.290.7427 fax
www.moso.com
Retail/wholesale.

Nikzad Import Inc.
538 N. La Cienega Blvd.
Los Angeles, CA 90048
866.333.6366
310.657.6662
310.657.6556 fax
www.nikzad.com
Retail/wholesale.

Plyboo America Inc.
745 Chestnut Ridge Rd.
Kirkville, NY 13082
315.687.3240
315.687.5177 fax
www.plyboo-america.com
Retail/wholesale.

* **Smith & Fong-Plyboo**
  601 Grandview Ave.
  So. San Francisco, CA 94080
  866.835.9859
  650.872.1184
  650.872.1185 fax
  www.plyboo.com
  Plyboo flooring, floating floor; retail/wholesale.

TimberGrass LLC
7995 N.E. Day Rd.
Bainbridge Island, WA 98110
800.929.6333
206.842.9477
206.842.9456 fax
www.timbergrass.com
Retail/wholesale.

Yucatan Bamboo
(See Furniture)
Retail.

International

Amati Bambu Ltd.
160 Bullock Dr.
Markham ON L3P 1W2
Canada
905.477.8899
905.477.5208 fax
www.amatibambu.com
Retail/wholesale.

China Bamboo Flooring
China Liu An Bamboo Product Co.
Lan Tian da lou, Jianqiao Rd.
Lin An City, Zhejiang Province
P.R. China 311300
86.571637.33416
86.571637.26372 fax
www.flooronline.net

Elephant Parkett GmBH
Dorfstr. 28
27726 Worpswede
Germany
0049.(0).4792.951.556
0049.(0).4792.951.558 fax
www.elephantparkett.de

MEWO Bambusparkett
H-Trade GmBH
Alte Landstrafe 1
D 97218 Gerbrunn
Germany
49.931.7059852
49.931.7059840 fax
www.bambus-parkett.de

Plyboo Bamboo Flooring Int'l
Dorpsweg 125
1697 KJ Schellinkhout
Netherlands
31.0.29.503500
31.0.229.501970 fax
www.plyboo.nl
Sportfloor.

Wellmade Wooden & Bamboo Products, Corp
18313 Hanzhongmen St. 210029
Nanjing, Jiangsu
P.R. China
86.25.652.8341
86.25.661.3758 fax
www.wellmadecorp.com
www.bamboofloorings.com

Bamboo Objects

USA

Ad Infinitum
3940 W. Cornelia Ave.
Chicago, IL 60618
773.539.0596
773.539.0662 fax
www.madeinthephilippines.com
Philippine wind and percussion, jews harp; retail.

Bamboo Mountain Imports
(See Furniture)
Crafts; retail.

Banana Joe's
1415 Abbot Kinney Blvd.
Venice, CA 90291
310.452.2343
310.450.1033 fax
Accessories; retail.

Bamboo Bike Co. LLC
503.650.5162
503.656.2503 fax
www.bamboobike.com
Bicycles; retail/wholesale.

Bamboo Flutes
501 Beverly Ave.
Capitola, CA 95010
831.476.2259
Shakuhachi, transverse.

Bamboo 54 Inc.
315 N. San Marino Ave.
San Gabriel, CA 91775
626.281.3780
626.281.3916 fax
www.bamboo54.com
Bicycles, housewares, clothing, handbags; retail.

Bamboo Nation
P.O. Box 1028
Cosmopolis, WA 98537
360.538.0160
www.bamboonation.org
Fresh shoots available to Western WA only. Cookbook, crafts; retail.

Bamboo Ride
253.761.9745
253.761.9746 fax
www.bambooride.anthill.com
Bicycles, tricycles; retail.

* **Cabana- Space 432**
432 State St.
Santa Barbara, CA 93101
805.963.4004
Housewares, accessories; clothing; retail. (Visit to see red umbrella on cover.)

Cherry Blossom Gardens
16159 320th St.
New Prague, MN 56071
877.226.4387
952.758.1922 fax
www.garden-gifts.com
Fountains.

Chateau Edgewater Inc.
P.O. Box 2436
Wilsonville, OR 97070
503.280.8070
503.280.8107 fax
www.edecor.com
Baskets, screens, trunks; retail.

Cost Plus World Imports
www.costplus.com

Fountain Finder
www.fountainfinder.com
Various bamboo fountains; retail.

* **Happy Horticulture**
(See Interior Finish Materials)
Hammocks, useful objects.

* **Imagine**
11 W. Canon Perdido
Santa Barbara, CA 93101
805.899.3700
Housewares, books, unusual useful objects, accessories; retail.

Lark in the Morning
P.O. Box 799
Fort Bragg, CA 95437
707.964.5569
707.964.1979 fax
www.larkinam.com
World bamboo instruments; retail.

* **Maienza Wilson Design Gallery**
(See Interior Designers)
Japanese baskets, crafts, fine art; retail.

* **Mingei Oriental Antiques**
736 State St.
Santa Barbara, CA 93101
805.963.3257
Fine arts and crafts; retail.

Lee Jofa
201 Central Ave. South
Bethpage, NY 11714
800.453.3563
www.e-designtrade.com
Bamboo print fabric; to the Trade.

Oriental Imports
P.O. Box 2430
Daphne, AL 36526
334.626.1049 tel/fax
Blinds and screens; retail.

Pier 1 Imports
(See Furniture)
Housewares, accessories.

* **Richard Waters**
P. O. Box 1071
Pahoa, HI 96778
808.965.0955
www.waterphone.com/bamboo.html
Unique bamboo instruments; retail.

Romy Benton
P.O. Box 10871
Portland, OR 97296
503.222.4067
www.romyb.com
Unique woodwinds; retail.

Smith + Noble
www.smithandnoble.com
Blinds; retail.

Sunreed Instruments
P.O. Box 389
220 Hidden Glen Rd.
Ascutney, VT 05030
802.674.9585 tel/fax
www.sunreed.com
Saxophones, clarinets, wind instruments, digeridoos; retail/wholesale.

Tallgrass Winds
553 S. Parkview Rd.
Nashville, TN 47448
812.988.2353
www.tallgrasswinds.com
Transverse flutes; retail.

Tai Gallery/Textile Arts
616-1/2 Canyon Rd.
Santa Fe, NM 87501
505.984.1387
505.989.7770 fax
www.textilearts.com/bamboo
Contemporary Japanese baskets; retail.

* **William Laman**
(See Furniture)
Housewares, accessories.

World Treasure Trading Co.
815 Piner Rd.
Santa Rosa, CA 95403
707.566.7888
707.566.7890 fax
Housewares; wholesale.

Yamaha Corp. of America
Buena Park, CA
714.522.9011
www.yamaha.com
Bamboo guitar; snare drums; retail.

International

A World of Bamboo
Buenos Aires, Argentina
54.11.4765.4820
http://usuarios.arnet.com.ar/bambu/
Einstruments.htm
Wind and percussion instruments; retail.

* **Bamboo Surfboards Australia**
84-86 Centennial Circuit
Byron Bay NSW 2841
New South Wales
Australia
61.2.6685.6804
61.2.6685.6257 fax
www.bamboosurfboards.com.au
Surfboards, skateboards; retail/wholesale.

Chinese Manubaskets Co.
10 Dongfeng Rd.
Qinzhou 535000
Guangxi, China
86.777.281.9853
86.777.281.0858 fax
www.cnbaskets.com/bamboo.htm
Baskets; retail.

Musica Bambusa
P.O. Box 178
Berry NSW 2535
Australia
61.02.4464.1336
www.shoal.net.au/~musicabam
*Wind, percussion instruments;
retail/wholesale.*

* **Tough Skins Bamboo
Surfboards
Goodtime**
29 Ipswich Rd.
Woollongabba,
Queensland 4102
Australia
07.3391.8588
07.3891.1029 fax
www.goodtime.com.au
Surfboards.

Outdoor Applications

Poles

* **Bamboo Craftsman Co.**
2819 N. Winchell
Portland, OR 97217
503.285.5339
www.bamboocraftsman.com
Retail.

Bamboo Depot
(See Indoor Applications - Interior
Finishes)

Bamboo 54 Inc.
(See Bamboo Objects)

* **Bamboo Gardener**
P.O. Box 17949
Seattle, WA 98107
206.782.3490
www.bamboogardener.com
Retail.

Bamboo Maui Inc.
(See Indoor Applications - Interior
Finishes)

Bamboo & Rattan Works, Inc.
(See Indoor Applications - Interior
Finishes)

Bamboo Supply Company
P.O. Box 5433
Lakeland, FL 33807
800.568.9087
863.646.8561 fax
Retail.

Benson's Import Corp.
(See Indoor Applications - Interior
Finishes)

Frank's Cane & Rush Supply
(See Indoor Applications - Interior
Finishes)

* **Livingreen**
218 Helena Ave.
Santa Barbara, CA 93101
805.966.1319
805.966.1309 fax
www.livingreen.com
Retail/wholesale.

Safari Thatch & Bamboo
(See Fences & Outdoor Structures)

Steve Ray's Bamboo Gardens
250 Cedar Cliff Rd.
Springville, AL 35146
205.594.3438
www.thebamboogardens.com
Retail.

Takeroku America
Groton, MA
877.692.3624
978.433.4951 fax
www.japanesebamboo.com
Retail.

The Bamboo Man
7810 SW 118th St.
Miami, FL 33156
305.378.9449
305.378.2018 fax
Retail.

Yucatan Bamboo
(See Indoor Applications - Interior
Finishes)

Fences and Outdoor Structures

Bamboo & Rattan Works
(See Indoor Applications - Interior Finishes)
Fencing.

* **Bamboo Craftsman Co.**
(See Poles)
Garden structures.

Bamboo Depot
(See Indoor Applications - Interior Finishes)
Fences and panels, gazebos.

* **Bamboo Fencer**
179 Boylston St.
Jamaica Plain, MA 02130
800.775.8641
617.524.6137
617.524.6100 fax
www.bamboofencer.com
Fences, fencing; retail.

Bamboo 54 Inc.
(See Bamboo Objects)

Bamboo Gardener
(See Poles)

* **Bamboo Giant Nursery**
5601 Freedom Blvd.
Aptos, CA 95003
831.687.0100
831.687.0200 fax
www.bamboogiant.com
Fencing; retail.

Bamboo Maui Inc.
(See Indoor Applications - Interior Finishes)
Fencing.

Bamboo Supply Co.
(See Poles)
Fencing.

Benson's Import Corp.
(See Indoor Applications - Interior Finishes)
Structures.

Fernau Hartman Architects
(See Designers - Architects)
Treehouses.

Frank's Cane & Rush Supply
(See Indoor Applications - Interior Finishes)
Structures.

Hammacher Schlemmer
800.233.4800
www.hammacherschlemmer.com
Thatched hut.

* **Island Ambiance**
459 Normal Ave.
Ashland, OR 97520
541.482.6357
http://netdial.caribe.net/~bamboo
Treehouses.

Safari Thatch & Bamboo Inc.
2036 C North Dixie Hwy
Ft. Lauderdale, FL 33305
954.564.0059
954.564.7431 fax
www.safarithatch.com
Structures and construction.

Takeroka America
(See Poles)
Gates, windows.

Bridges and Site Sculpture

USA

Bamboo Depot
(See Interior Finishes)
Bridges.

* **Michael McDonough**
(See Furniture)
Custom bridge.

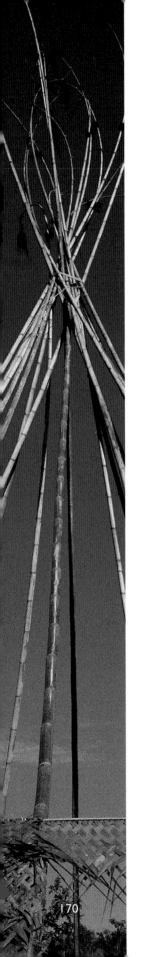

* **Stephen Glassman**
703 Palms Blvd.
Venice, CA 90291
310.305.1696
310.578.5189 fax
www.izome.com
Custom bridges, fences, site-specific sculptures.

* **Steven Rosenthal**
511 Analu St.
Honolulu, HI 96817
808.595.4714
bambuta@aol.com
Site-specific sculptures.

International

Akio Hizume, architect
81.274.87.2828 fax
http://homepage1.nifty.com/starcage/
englishindex.html
"Star Cage" sculptures.

* **Antoon Versteegde**
Millsebaan 42
NL - 5402 LW Uden
The Netherlands
0.031.413.260.013
www.antoonversteegde.nl
Site sculptures.

* **Jörg Stamm, engineer**
Calle 5 #0-80
Popayan, Cauca, Colombia
57.2.824.4438
jstamm@emtel.net.co
Custom bridges.

Tools and Supplies

* **Bamboo Craftsman Co.**
(See Outdoor Applications - Poles)

* **Bamboo Gardener**
(See Bamboo Objects)

Bamboo Gardens of Washington
5016 192nd Pl.
Redmond, WA 98074
425.868.5166
425.868.5360 fax
www.BambooGardensWA.com
Craft tools; retail/wholesale.

* **Bamboo-Smiths**
P.O. Box 1801
Nevada City, CA 95959
530.292.9449
530.292.9460 fax
tbs@sierratimberframers.com
Saws, splitting and carving knives, miscellaneous supplies; retail.

* **Hida Tools**
1333 San Pablo Ave.
Berkeley, CA 94702
800.443.5512
510.524.3700
510.524.3423 fax
www.hidatool.com
Saws, knives, splitters, bits; retail.

Hirade America
51 Shattuck Ave.
Pepperell, MA 01463
877.692.3624
978.433.4951 fax
www.japanesetools.com
Bamboo woodworking tools from Japan: saws, chisels, splitters, thread makers.

Misugi Designs
707.422.0734
707.425.2465 fax
www.misugidesigns.com
Japanese woodworking tools; retail.

The Japan Woodworker
1731 Clement Ave.
Alameda, CA 94501
800.537.7820
www.japanwoodworker.com
Japanese saws, knives, splitters, rope; retail.

* **Tradewinds Bamboo Nursery**
(See Nurseries)
Tools.

Notes

Bibliography

Books

Austin, Robert, Dana Levy, and Koichiro Ueda. *Bamboo*. New York: Weatherhill, 1970.

Bell, Michael. *The Gardener's Guide to Growing Temperate Bamboos*. Portland, Oregon: Timber Press, 2000.

Beng, Tan Hock. *Tropical Architecture and Interiors: Tradition-based Design of Indonesia, Malaysia, Singapore, Thailand*. Singapore: Page One Publishing PTE LTD, 1994.

Bess, Nancy Moore, with Bibi Wein. *Bamboo in Japan*. New York: Kodansha International, 2001.

Coffland, Robert T. *Contemporary Japanese Bamboo Arts*. Chicago: Art Media Resources, 1999.

Crowley, James and Sandra. *Wabi Sabi Style*. Salt Lake City, Utah: Gibbs Smith, Publisher, 2001.

Cusak, Victor. *Bamboo World*. Sydney: Kangaroo Press, 1999.

Dethier, Jean, Walter Liese, Frei Otto, Eda Schaur, and Klaus Steffens. *Grow Your Own House: Simón Vélez and Bamboo Architecture*. Weil-am-Rhein, Germany: Vitra Design Museum/ZERI/C.I.R.E.C.A., 2000.

Dunkleberg, Klaus. *IL 31: Bambus Bamboo/Bamboo as a Building Material/Building with Vegetal Rods*. Stuttgart, Germany: Information of the Institute for Lightweight Structures (IL) No. 31, 1985.

Elizabeth, Lynne, and Cassandra Adams, eds. *Alternative Construction: Contemporary Natural Building Methods*. New York: Wiley & Sons, 2000.

Farrelly, David. *The Book of Bamboo*. San Francisco: Sierra Club Books, 1984.

Janssen, Jules J. A. *Building with Bamboo*. London: Intermediate Technology Publications, 1998.

Judziewicz, Emmet J., Lynn Clark, Ximena Londoño, and Margaret Stern. *American Bamboos*. Washington, D.C.: Smithsonian Institution Press, 1999.

Kaley, Vinoo. *Venu Bharati: A Comprehensive Volume on Bamboo*. Maharashtra, India: Aproop Nirman Publisher, 2000.

Koren, Leonard. *Wabi-Sabi for Artists, Designers, Poets, and Philosophers*. Berkeley: Stone Bridge Press, 1994.

Liese, Walter. *The Anatomy of Bamboo Culms—Technical Report 18*. Beijing: International Network for Bamboo and Rattan (INBAR), 1998.

Liese, Walter. *Bamboos: Biology, Silvics, Properties, Utilization*. Eschborn, Germany: Deutsche Gessellschaft für Technische Zusammenarbeit (GTZ) GmBH, 1985.

López, Oscar Hidalgo. *Manual de Construcción con Bambú (Manual for Constructing with Bamboo)*. Bogotá: Estudios Tecnicos Colombianos Ltda, 1981.

McClure, F. A. *The Bamboos*. Washington, D.C.: Smithsonian Institution Press, 1993.

Meredith, Ted Jordan. *Bamboo for Gardens*. Portland, Oregon: Timber Press, 2001.

Oster, Maggie. *Bamboo Baskets*. New York: Viking Studio Books, 1995.

Recht, Christine, and Max Wetterwald. *Bamboos*. Portland, Oregon: Timber Press, 1992.

Stangler, Carol A. *The Craft and Art of Bamboo*. New York: Lark Books, 2001.

Starsota, Paul, and Yves Crouzet. *Bamboos*. Köln, Germany: Evergreen, 1998.

Suziki, Osamu, and Isao Yoshikawa. *Bamboo Fences of Japan*. Tokyo: Graphic-Sha Publishing Co., 1988.

Tierney, Lennox. *Wabi Sabi: A New Look at Japanese Design*. Salt Lake City, UT: Gibbs Smith, Publisher, 1999.

Villegas, Marcelo. *Tropical Bamboo*. Bogotá: Villegas+Editores, 1996.

Yoshikawa, Isao. *Japanese Gardening in Small Spaces*. Tokyo: Japan Publications Trading Co. Ltd., 1996.

Articles

*Indicates articles about growing bamboos.

Adkins, Dorcas. "Make Your Own Tabletop Tsukubai." Adapted from book *Simple Fountains for Indoors and Outdoors; Natural Home*, March/April 2000, 46–47.

Alexander, Judith. "Bamboo." *Metropolitan Home*, November 1996.

_____. "Bamboozled!" *McCall's*, March 2001, 104–106.

* Beck, Pam. "Perennially Yours—Do You Bamboo? Better think twice." *The News & Observer*, Raleigh, NC, July 2001, sec. 1E.

Bernstein, Fred. "Living la dolce vita," *Metropolitan Home*, July/August 2001, 132–135.

Breckenridge, Mary Beth. "Exotic Bamboo Stronger, More Stable than Traditional Flooring." *Santa Barbara News-Press*, 8 July 2001, sec. E23.

Bussel, Abby. "Bamboo Box." *Interior Design*, June 2001, 168–172.

Carrier, Susan. "The Bamboo Brothers." *Los Angeles Times*, 26 March 2000, sec. E2.

Casanave, Suki. "Treehouses—Growing Wild and Branching Out." *Architectural Record*, April 2001, 104–108.

Charpenter, Bruce. "The Queen of Bamboo—an Interview with Linda Garland." *Bali Echo*, 1994, 10–13.

Cheng, Scarlet. "Weaving a Web of Natural Grace." *Los Angeles Times*, Calendar, 29 July 2001, 53.

Clark, Milo. "Bamboo as a Community Resource: Bamboo as an Industrial Commodity." *Sustainability Living News* 17, Fall 1998.

Clark, Milo. "Being with Bamboo." American Bamboo Society Website, August 2001.

Clark, Milo. "Venu Bharti, Wabi Sabi, and IL 31." Unpublished, August 2001.

* Conover, Adele. "A New World Comes to Life, Discovered in a Stalk of Bamboo." *Smithsonian*, October 1994, 121–128.

DeBoer, Darrel. "The Architecture of Simón Vélez." Unpublished, 2000.

DeBoer, Darrel, and Karl Bareis. "Bamboo Building and Culture." Unpublished, 2000.

_____. "How Do You Make It Green?— Interview with Darrel DeBoer." *Dwell*, June 2001, 90–91.

Estrada, Andrea. "New surfboard design offered." *Santa Barbara News-Press*, 8 August 1999, sec. F3.

Estrada, Andrea. "Style and Sensibilities with Feng Shui." *Santa Barbara News-Press*, 15 April 2001, sec. E20-21.

Frankel, Elana. "The Future—Will Bamboo, An Ecologically Sound Alternative and Renewable Resource, Become the Norm?" *Architectural Record*, April 1998.

Goldberg, Gale Beth. "Building with Bamboo." *The Newsletter of the Sustainability Project* 4, no.1, April 2000, 12–13.

Goldberg, Gale Beth. "Iron Grass, Vegetable Steel—The Architecture of Simón Vélez and Marcelo Villegas in Colombia, South America." Self-published, December 1999.

Greenspan, Emily Newman. "Bamboozled." *Shop Talk—Newel Art Galleries*, November-December 1998.

Haldeman, Peter. "Carving Out a Niche on Bali— A Designer Sculpts Her Indonesian Landscape." *Architectural Digest*, March 1994, 94–103.

* Hammond, Judy. "Bamboo—Tips on Caring for Bamboo." *Santa Barbara News-Press*, 12 August 1999, sec. D1, 3.

* Hayes, Virginia, "The Well-Behaved Bamboo—Clumpers Good, Runners Bad: How to Tell the Difference." *The Santa Barbara Independent*, 13 September 2001, 35.

Heeger, Susan. "Raising Cane—a Bamboo Grower with a Passion for Plants and Pit Bulls." *Los Angeles Times, Magazine*, 16 August 1998, 31.

Hellman, Peter. "Design 100—Design that Makes a Difference: #64 Darrel DeBoer." *Metropolitan Home*, March/April 2001, 90.

Hirst, Arlene. "Q: Can this Kitchen Be Saved?" *Metropolitan Home*, May/June 2001, 96, 99, 100.

Huber, Jeanne. "The Stalk Market." *This Old House*, no. 31, September 1999.

Interlante, Christine. "Eco-sensible Eco-nomics—Why Bamboo is Good Business." *Garuda*, May 1995, 13–15.

_____, "Is Bamboo for You?" *Consumer Reports*, February 2001, 47.

Kwaschik, Ralf. "INBAR Electronic Discussion Groups." *Bamboo—The Magazine of the American Bamboo Society*, August 2001, 7.

Liese, Walter. "Opportunities and Constraints for Processing and Utilization of Bamboo and Rattan in North-East India." Paper presented at the International Fund for Agricultural Development—Workshop on Bamboo and Rattan Project in North-East India, Rome, 22–23 February 2001.

Madden, Chris Casson. "Bamboo's Popularity Shoots Up." *Raleigh News & Observer*, 10 February 2001.

Marden, Luis. "Bamboo, the Giant Grass." *National Geographic*, October 1980.

McCausland, Jim. "Building with Bamboo." *Sunset*, July 1994, 86–90.

* Miles, Carol, Chen Chuhe, and Tamera Flores. "On-Farm Bamboo Production in the Pacific Northwest." *Bamboo—The Magazine of The American Bamboo Society*, August 2001, 12.

Miller, Molly. "Bamboo Running." *Natural Home*, March/April 2000, 40–45.

Moed, Andrea. "Bamboozler—Designer Michael McDonough Keeps Finding New Ways to Use the Grass That Is Stronger Than Steel." *Metropolis*, June 1998.

Morrison, Lynn. "Bamboo Shoots to New Popularity." Special to *Interiors*, 29 August 1996; *The Sacramento Bee*, 1997.

_____. "Nova OnLine: Secrets of the Lost Empire—China Bridge; Nova Builds a Rainbow Bridge." Nova Website, November 2000.

* Orr, Stephen. "Dig It." *House & Garden*, June 2001, 50.

_____. "Introduction." *Parade of Green Buildings* pamphlet. Santa Barbara, CA: The Sustainability Project and the Santa Barbara Contractors Association, October 2000, 5.

Pearson, David. "Home Sweet Treehouse—How to Live in a Treehouse." *Mother Earth* News, August/September 2001, 23–33.

Phinney, Susan. "Bamboo Isn't Just for Window Blinds Anymore; Now It's for Floors, Too." *Seattle Post-Intelligencer*, 3 November 2001.

* Pokorny, Kim. "Bamboo Rising—The Asian Import Stakes Out New Territory." *The Oregonian, Homes and Gardens of the Northwest*, 13 September 2001.

Pollack, Andrew. "One Defense Against Quakes: Build Homes of Wood." *New York Times, Week in Review*, 31 January 1999, 5.

Prisant, Carol. "Bamboo." *Martha Stewart Living*, October 1997, 186–193.

Riggio, Tod. "Stronger—Than—Steel: Bamboo Gets a New Look." *Woodshop News*, July 1998.

Robledo, J. E., J. F. Munoz, and Gonzalo Ducre. "Colombian Bamboo Society—Bamboo (Bahareque) House and the Manizales, Colombia Earthquake." *Southern California Bamboo*, July 1999, 6–7.

Shulman, Ken. "Green Building: Knock on Wood—Will a Bamboo Pavilion from Colombia Stand Up to German Building Codes?" *Metropolis*, April 2000, 52.

* Smaus, Robert. "In the Garden—Blocking with Bamboo." *Los Angeles Times*, 2 November 2000, sec. E1, E4.

Sorvig, Kim. "Bamboo Magic." *RHS Monthly*, July 1983, 269–271.

Stager, Phillip J. "Bamboo and Philately." *The Journal of the American Bamboo Society* 14, no. 1, 1999, 6–22.

* Steadman, Todd A. "Bamboo." *Landscape Architecture*, February 1999, 74–76.

Stein, Jeannine. "Design 2000: Going Beyond the Tiki Hut." *Los Angeles Times*, 31 August 2000, sec. E1.

Steinfeld, Carol. "A Bamboo Future." *Environmental Design and Construction*, September/October 1998, 32–35.

Stevens, Jane. "Bamboo is Back." *International Wildlife*, January/February 1995, 38–44.

Stewart, Martha. "Versatility of Bamboo Is Downright Bamboozling." *Santa Barbara News-Press*, 27 May 1999, sec. D3.

Strickland, Ellen. "Grass Comes Inside: Bamboo Flooring in Your Home." *Healing Retreats and Spas*, February/March 2001, 62–65.

Vendrenne, Elisabeth. "Charlotte Perriand: The Enlightened Militant of Post-War Modernity." *Intramuros*, April/May 2000.

Viladas, Pilar. "This Side of Paradise—Balinese Elements Accent a House on Fiji." *Architectural Digest*, September 1994, 80–91.

Westbrook, Leslie. "Hip and Green." *Food & Home*, Spring 2001, 61.

Whiteley, Peter O. "Nature's Own Flooring." *Sunset*, April 2001, 148–152.

Wood, Chris. "Totally Floored." *Custom Home*, January/February 2001, 90–92.

Young, Emily. "Poles Apart—An Artist Envisions a Future Built of Bamboo." *Los Angeles Times Magazine*, 7 May 2000, 27–29..

Photograph and Illustration Credits

Key: Top=t, Bottom=b, Right=r, Left=l, Middle=m

© Paul Avis: 30 tl, 99, 121 all

© The Bamboo Fencer, Inc.: 1, 40 tr, 68-69, 112-13, 117 t, 139, 169

© The Budji Collections, Inc.: 77 b

Courtesy of Bamboo-Smiths, © Bill Schwob: 140 all

Courtesy of Bamboo Technologies: 27 r, 63

Courtesy of Nancy Moore Bess: 134 b

Courtesy of Charissa Brock, © John Woodin: 73 b

© Susan Burns: 50 t

Courtesy of Gary Chafe, © James Chen: 71 tl

© Frank Chang: 118-19

Courtesy of Dorothy Churchill-Johnson: 71 mr

© Hazel Colditz: 73 t

© Christopher Covey: 76 b, 101

© Grey Crawford: 81 r

© Darrel DeBoer: 56-57, 142 (1-6), 143 (1-5), 144 all, 145 tl

© Shari Arai DeBoer: 70

© D. James Dee: 71 b

© Christopher Dow: 74-75, 80-81

Courtesy of Wolfgang Eberts, © Max Felix Wetterwald: 8-9

© Christophe Ellis: 110-111

© Gale Beth Goldberg: 2, 5 r, 7 r, 9, 10, 11, 12, 13, 16, 17, 20, 23, 24, 28, 30 b, 33 all, 34 bm, 36 bl and br, 37 tl and r, 40 bl, 41, 42 t, 42-43 br, 43 l, 44-45 all, 46-47, 49, 50 b, 58-59 all, 60 all, 61 all, 64, 65, 66, 67 t, 76 t, 83 all, 86 all, 88 l, 94, 97, 100, 102 all, 103 all, 104 b, 107 b, 108, 109, 114 all, 115, 124 r, 129 bl, 130, 137, 141 all, 142 br, 143 bm (6) (7), 144-45 br, 156, 157, 162, 165, 170, 174; illustrations: 127, 128, 129, 131, 133, 134, 135, 136

© Larry Dale Gordon: 78, 90, 106, 107 t

© Calvin Hashimoto: 37 bl, 72 r, 82

© Laura Hull: 124 l

© David Joseph: 87, 92-93 all, 154

© Kevin Lang: 40 br

© Albert Lewis: 32, 88-89

© Walter Liese: 18 l, 31, 35 tr, 46 l, 51, 55, 74 l, 112 l, 138, 161

© Susanne Lucas: 4-5, 14, 15, 22, 48, 67 b, 123, 125, 126, 129 r, 148-49, 166

© Peter Malinowski/InSite: 96, 104 t, 105

© Wayne McCall: 21, 25

Courtesy of Michael McDonough, © Roy Wright: 29 all

© Gerard Minakawa: 145 bm and r (2), 146 all, 147 all

Courtesy of Newel Art Galleries: 52, 53, 54

Courtesy of Pier 1 Imports: 30 tr, 77 tr, 95, 153

© Joshua Rosenbaum: 6-7, 36 t, 38-39, 42 bl, 158

© Cesar Rubio: 122

© Jo Scheer: 35 b

© Daniel Smith: 18-19, 26-27 b, 34 tl, 35 tl, 85

© Jörg Stamm: 34 tr, 116 all

Courtesy of Jill Vander Hoof: 72 l

© Kristen Weber: 79

Courtesy of Wright Way Organic Resource Center: 117 b